A colour guide to familiar
MOUNTAIN FLOWERS

A colour guide to familiar

MOUNTAIN FLOWERS

By Bohumil Slavík

Illustrated by Jiřina Kaplická

Translated by Olga Kuthanová
Graphic design: Soňa Valoušková
Line drawings: Michal Skalník

English version first published 1977 by
Octopus Books Limited
59 Grosvenor Street, London W 1

© 1977 Artia, Prague

ISBN 0 7064 0672 9

Printed in Czechoslovakia
3/10/16/51-01

CONTENTS

FOREWORD

The boundless creative force of the elements produced the remarkable world of high mountains. For millions of years they moulded the Earth, forming its principal features, the oceans and the continents. The majesty of the high peaks, covered with eternal snow and veiled by the clouds, made the mountains the home of the gods, esteemed and feared by mankind for centuries. Man, however, was forever trying to discover their secrets, and to understand their plant and animal life. He collected, investigated, described and classified. He came to know not only individual species but whole communities of living organisms, plants and animals as well as the relationships between them and their environment. Much is already known, but much still remains to be learned.

Every trip into the mountains brings within reach the colourful beauty of the plant world. The diversity and richness of colour and the elegance of form delights and enchants everybody. A trip from the valley to the snowline, 3,000 to 4,000 m above sea-level, is effectively the same as a journey of 1,000 km or so to the Arctic Circle and beyond. The climate from lowland to high altitude changes in much the same manner as with geographical zones when passing from warm regions to arctic tundra. As a matter of fact, many plant species which grow in high mountains are also to be found in the northern tundra. It is the aim of this book to acquaint the reader with the life of high-mountain plants, the unusual aspects of their environment, the necessity of protecting them and, above all, preventing their disappearance from the face of the Earth.

HOW HIGH MOUNTAINS EVOLVED

Science long ago banished the many tales and legends about the creation of mountains by supernatural forces. That man created these tales and legends, however, is not surprising for he saw mountains not only as vast masses of hard stone but sometimes he may have witnessed the growth of volcanoes which even to this day remain a continual source of wonder.

The Earth's crust is in constant motion. The movements are barely perceptible; they are measured in centimetres or at most metres per year, both in the vertical as well as the horizontal plane. For example, Scandinavia is rising by about one centimetre a year; the mountains of Japan and of the Pacific

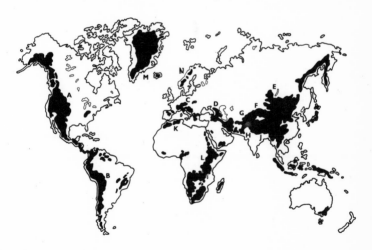

Fig. 1. Principal high-mountain systems of the world
A — Cordilleras, Rocky Mountains   B — Andes   C — Alps   D — Caucasus   E — Altai   F — Tien Shan   G — Pamir   H — Hindu Kush   J — Himalayas   K — Atlas   L — East African mountains   M — Greenland   N — Scandinavian mountains

islands rise by 0.5 m to 1 m a year. Iceland, Greenland and North America are drifting away from Europe by several metres each year and the same is true of Madagascar. In the particular geological periods, however, there are marked orogenic or mountain-forming events. In most cases several hundred million years have passed between the principal mountain-forming periods on the Earth's surface.

At certain times the pressures and forces hidden deep inside the Earth are released. These result in the formation of mountains, either by the folding of the Earth's crust or by faulting or by volcanic activity. There were, of course, relatively calm periods between the individual mountain-forming phases.

Of the main orogenic periods, at least three should be mentioned. The Caledonian orogenesis occurred in the Paleozoic era in the Ordovician, Silurian and Devonian periods, when mountains were formed in Norway, the greater part of England, Scotland and Ireland and in Holland, Germany and elsewhere. The Variscian (Hercynian) orogenesis occurred mainly in the Carboniferous-Permian period and raised the mountains running from central France across Normandy to Cornwall and from central France to central Europe. The third and last, and most important in regard to the European high mountains as we know them today, was the Alpine orogenesis which took place from the end of the Triassic period, through the whole of the Tertiary and up to the beginning of the Quaternary. This was the period which saw the uplifting of the Pyrenees, the Apennines, the Alps, the Carpathians, the Balkan ranges, the southern Crimea, the Caucasus, the mountains of Asia Minor and the Middle East and the Himalayas.

When climbing these mountain giants they will seem as though they have been like this since the beginning of time, but how different are the facts! There were periods in the Earth's history when there may have been a shallow sea where they now stand; perhaps one day they will be supplanted by flat, spreading lake country. We have to learn that mountains are born, grow, age and die.

CHARACTERISTIC FEATURES
OF HIGH-MOUNTAIN PLANTS

Nature decked the high-mountain regions above the upper timber line with a wonderful array of flowers. These regions are covered with snow for a long time — often until early summer — and then become carpeted with alpine turf or covered with rubble and occasional clumps of flowers. Trees cannot grow in this region; only peaks covered with permanent ice and snow can be seen. This colourful world of plants has its individualities. Climate, soil and other factors are so distinctive that their long-term influences have selected particular plant species.

The higher the altitude, the lower the mean annual temperature. Decrease in temperature means a longer snow cover and therefore a shorter growing season, i.e. a period of time

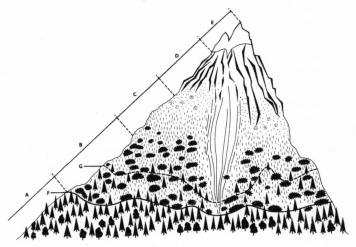

Fig. 2. Schematic representation of altitudinal levels in the high mountains
A — mountain belt B — subalpine belt C — alpine belt D — below the
snow line E — the snow zone F — upper forest limit G — tree line

with a favourable climate, allowing the undisturbed course of plant growth. Above the upper timber line the flowering period lasts about three months. This must suffice for high-mountain plants to flower, produce seeds and, in certain instances, to form new flower buds for the following year's growth.

Some species start to flower as soon as the snow melts. They need only a few days in a favourable temperature for them to produce blossoms from the previous year's buds. Among the first to blossom in this way on the alpine meadows and screes are *Crocus vernus, Bulbocodium vernum, Soldanella alpina* and *S. pusilla, Primula auricula, Hutchinsia alpina, Saxifraga oppositifolia, Pulsatilla vernalis, Draba aizoides, Viola calcarata, Gentiana verna, Narcissus poeticus* and several others. In the Pamirs, for example, *Sibbaldia tetrandra* flowers 5 to 10 days after the snow has melted and bears fruits 25 to 30 days later. However, plants do not develop at the same rate at all altitudes; they mature more rapidly as altitude increases. The difference in the rate of development with each 100 m of altitude is termed the phenological gradient. This is markedly variable. In the Caucasus, for example, the difference is practically immeasurable between altitudes of 1,300 to 2,000 m. At 2,000 to 2,400 m it averages 5 to about 7.5 days for every 100 m of height; at higher altitudes it again decreases. For example *Pulsatilla albana* flowered 31 days after the onset of the growing season at an altitude of 1,950 m. On the other hand, flowering took place after 11 days at 2,400 m, after 14 days at 2,700 m and after 23 days at 3,000 m. The same is true for the ripening of the seeds. It has been found that the most favourable conditions, apparently caused by the optimum combination of temperature and day-length, are at the upper limit of the sub-alpine level. Flowering, however, is greatly influenced, also, by the position of the slopes on which the plants grow. On north-facing slopes the growth cycle is naturally much delayed. Even a single tuft of mountain thrift such as *Armeria alpina* flowers several days later on a northern as distinct from a southern slope.

More than 90 per cent of high-mountain species are adapted to the short growth period. The remainder take longer to develop, so that only in some years do the seeds ripen; otherwise they multiply by vegetative means. Generally, many alpine species produce viable seeds much more regularly in high-mountain conditions. Moreover, they exhibit increased flowering and fruiting properties. Sometimes a woody plant transferred from lower localities will begin to bear fruit remarkably early in its life cycle, even within a few years.

A great majority of plants growing above the upper timber line are herbaceous perennials. Mostly they are hemicryptophytes with winter buds at the soil surface protected by their own leaves and snow; or they are chamaephytes with winter buds up to 30 cm above the soil surface and also protected by snow. Annuals are rare, comprising no more than four per cent of the high-mountain flora and completely absent at the highest elevations. Best known annual high-mountain plants are members of the *Endotricha* section of the genus *Gentiana, Sedum annuum* and *S. atratum,* all members of the semi-parasitic genus *Euphrasia.* Some species normally annual at lowland elevations are perennial in high altitude conditions.

The alpine climate is therefore apparently unfavourable for annuals; yet many herbaceous perennials, sub-shrubs and shrubs grow to a ripe old age in these harsh conditions. For example, the mountain avens *(Dryas octopetala),* a richly branched, white-flowering shrub, reaches 50 years of age in the Alps and up to 100 in the Arctic. Similarly, the dwarf juniper *(Juniperus communis* ssp. *nana)* and the alpine rose *(Rhododendron ferrugineum)* can grow to an age of over 100 years in the Alps. The annual rings on these woody plants are at most several hundredths of a millimetre in width. In the Pamirs some plants are estimated to be 200 to 300 years old or even more — for instance, the cushion-forming *Acantholimon diapensioides* and *Sibbaldia tetrandra,* plants which do not begin flowering until 15 to 25 years after germination. Most herbaceous perennials do not live so long but can survive for 20 to 60 years.

The majority of high-mountain species do not have deep roots because the soil layer is generally thin. There are continual and adequate supplies of water and moreover the top parts of the plants are also affected by frequent mists, rain and snow. In rare instances, however, the roots of some plants may grow to a considerable length. These are mainly in those species which grow in coarse rubble with nourishing fine soil washed deep down between the boulders and particles of rock. In some species those parts of the plant which are underground serve as a store for the large quantities of food which it needs for rapid development at the start of its short growing period. One such example is *Rheum maximowiczii* in the Pamirs; the rhizomes of a single specimen may weigh up to 30 or 40 kg.

The large and brightly coloured flowers of mountain plants attract insects. Of course, these are not common at higher elevations and they become fewer with each increase in altitude above the tree line. Despite the rarity of insect pollinations, there are many more entomophilous (insect pollinated) than anemophilous (wind pollinated) plants in high mountain meadows and screes. This may be because the irregular and often gale force winds do not promote successful pollination. The alpine flora normally consists of more than 80 per cent of entomophilous species; the remainder, mostly plants with insignificant, often greenish flowers, are anemophilous. Only at lower elevations do anemophilous plants constitute a greater part of the vegetation.

The flowers of mountain plants are often larger than those of related species growing at lower elevations. This has sometimes been explained as an optical illusion caused by the fact that the green parts of the plant were smaller — for example, a shorter stem and smaller leaves due to the harsh climate. This, however, is true only in certain instances.

Every visitor to mountain heights is enchanted by the colourful splendour of the flowers. Those who for the first time see the rock speedwell *(Veronica fruticans)* are likely to say that it is the loveliest shade of blue in the world; the sight of rock scorpion-grass *(Myosotis alpestris)* may evoke the same response. But this will be only if they have not previously marvelled at the glorious deep azure blue of the spring gentian *(Gentiana verna)*, the steely blue-violet of marsh felwort *(Swertia perennis)* or the pale blue-violet of the bellflower *(Campanula cenisia)*. For those interested in the numerical relationship of species and colour it may come as a surprise to learn that at the top of the list are the white-flowered species, followed in order by yellow, red, blue and violet. The green vegetative plant parts may sometimes be of a purple-green colour and not pure green, particularly with plants not covered by snow in winter. Such coloration has its beneficial aspects in view of the greater intensity of irradiation with large amounts of ultraviolet rays. Similarly the flowers of some plants have extra protective pigments; for example lowland relatives have yellow blossoms while the alpine species are coloured orange or reddish-orange. Spectacular examples include the golden hawkweed *(Hieracium aurantiacum)*, *Senecio abrotanifolius*, *Crepis aurea*, bird's foot trefoil *(Lotus corniculatus)*, and others. So too, instead of the white flowers which some species have at lowland elevations, in the mountains they have pink, violet-tinged or purple blossoms, e.g. *Ligusticum mutellina*, burnet saxifrage *(Pimpinella saxifraga)*, the mountain valerians *(Valeriana montana, V. tripteris* and *V. supina)* and round-leaved penny cress *(Thlaspi rotundifolium)*.

The adverse alpine climatic conditions have produced a number of remarkable adaptations in most plant species. Most striking, perhaps, is the growth of many herbaceous plants and shrubs to form cushions, mats and carpets in the crevices of otherwise bare rocks. *Saxifraga squarrosa* and *S. bryoides* form masses resembling thick fur; *Androsace helvetica* and *Saxifraga caesia* make solid domes seemingly completely air-tight. In fact, the temperature inside these tufts is much higher and more constant than that of the surrounding air. Snow melts sooner on these dense, compact tufts and it is therefore no wonder that they burst into bloom with myriads of tiny blossoms shortly after the beginning of the growing season. The intensive ultraviolet radiation at heights of several thousand metres retards the effect of the plant growing hormone auxin so that stem growth is slow, internodes are short and branching is prolific. Dwarfing is caused not only by ultraviolet radiation but also by low temperatures, markedly different diurnal temperatures, as well as by the influence of wind and snow. Slow growth can be observed not only in herbaceous but also in woody plants above the tree line. The higher the altitude, the smaller becomes the dwarf pine *(Pinus mugo)*, the dwarf juniper *(Juniperus communis* ssp. *nana)*, the dwarf birch *(Betula nana)* and the alpine rhododendrons *(Rhododendron ferrugineum* and *R. hirsutum)*. At the highest levels the layman is hard put to distinguish between the woody and the herbaceous perennial plants. Various willows, such as *Salix herbacea, S. reticulata, S. retusa* and others, grow close to the ground, almost prostrate — a far cry from their huge relatives of riverside woods and lowlands.

A distinctive character of high-montane flora is the large percentage of evergreen plants. This is a very important factor, for the plants can begin photosynthetic activity, i.e. they can commence to form those new organic substances necessary for growth immediately after the snow has melted. Photosynthesis takes place mostly in the leaves, so that evergreen plants are spared that time delay, which occurs in other plants before the formation of the first leaves, and which uses up much of the precious food store. Moreover, with evergreen plants photosynthesis may sometimes take place on warm, sunny days in winter, even under a thin layer of snow, for the lowest temperature limit at which it can occur is close to freezing point. Plants growing in places where the snow persists for a long time have a much higher chlorophyll content than plants growing in other habitats. Evergreen species in-

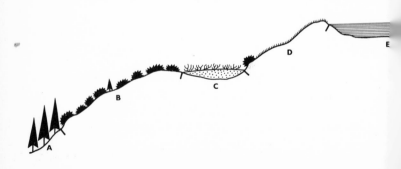

clude both woody and herbaceous plants, e.g. the rhododendrons, *Rhododendron ferrugineum* and *R. hirsutum,* the dwarf pine *(Pinus mugo),* the dwarf juniper *(Juniperus communis* ssp. *nana),* the trailing azalea *(Loiseleuria procumbens),* the arctic bearberry *(Arctostaphylos uva-ursi),* the mountain avens *(Dryas octopetala),* various houseleeks, most gentians and saxifrages as well as many grasses and sedges.

In places exposed to strong winds plants are liable to excessive evaporation. The leaves of many species are therefore

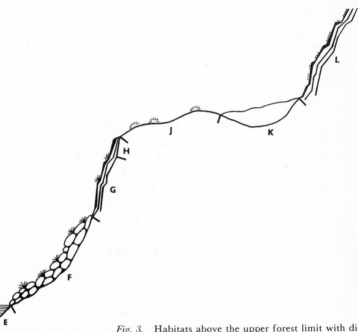

Fig. 3. Habitats above the upper forest limit with diverse plant formations

A — mountain forest   B — dwarf pine
C — peat bog   D — alpine turf
E — tarn   F — scree   G — rock crevices
H — high plateaux   J — cushion plants
K — snow field   L — rocks with lichens

adapted to such extreme conditions. Other problems of adaptation include survival in low temperatures and the lack of adequate mineral nutrients. In response to these conditions the leaf surface is either small and needle-like as with dwarf pines, junipers, the crowberry *(Empetrum)* and heaths *(Erica* species), or the leaves are broad but leathery and rigid. The leathery character is generally not produced by 'sclerenchyma' thickening up within the leaf but by the formation of thick outer layers on the leaf epidermis. Examples of plants with this type of leaf are the rhododendrons, members of the genera *Arctostaphylos* and *Dryas,* and the milkwort *(Polygala chamaebuxus)*. All adaptations tending to reduce transpiration are of particular importance in the case of tall plants where they are not covered by snow (dwarf pine, rhododendron), or are exposed to strong winds which prevent the formation of snow cover, for example, mountain avens *(Dryas octopetala),* the three-leaved rush *(Juncus trifidus)* and the sedge *(Carex firma).*

Many plants would freeze without snow cover and their resistance to freezing temperatures is very low. It is paradoxical that certain alpine species which are protected by winter snow cover may be killed by the first dry frost when transplanted to lowland elevations.

In view of their brief growing season montane plants must rapidly develop their vegetative and reproductive organs, as well as the foundations for the following year's growth. An important factor is the high rate of photosynthesis. Measurements taken on sunny days in the Alps show that some species absorb 18 to 27 mg of carbon dioxide per 100 cm^2 of leaf surface; in the mountains of central Asia this could exceed 50 mg, whereas in similar lowland species the amounts are often far less than 20 mg. The geographical location of the high-mountain ranges also has an effect. In a continental climate the photosynthetic process is much more active than in moist, suboceanic conditions. This increased rate of photosynthesis provides a greater concentration of sugar in the cell sap when temperatures fall; this, with the concurrently increased osmotic pressure enabling it to absorb water from the cold soil through the roots, protects the plant from freezing. Moreover, the high sugar and starch content of the leaves is important from an economic point of view, for such plants provide high quality grazing.

Wind and mountains are inseparable. Most days are windy and no breeze is likely to be gentle; on the contrary, winds are often fierce and prolonged. Only particularly hardy species such as the three-leaved rush *(Juncus trifidus)*, the sedges *(Carex firma* and *C. curvula), Elyna myosuroides, Kobresia simpliciuscula, Oreochloa disticha,* mountain avens *(Dryas octopetala)* and *Loiseleuria procumbens,* are likely to survive. These are either herbaceous plants forming dense, compact tufts or prostrate shrubs anchored firmly to the ground. Even these are not spared when their roots are exposed.

The velocity of winds in the mountains can be formidable. In central Europe the highest measured velocity is 40 to 50 m per second, in the arctic regions around 80 m per second has been recorded, and on mountain ridges the speeds are often more than 100 m per second. Worst to suffer are the shrubs and trees at the upper tree line. The constant swaying of weaker stems and branches limits their nourishment and in consequence the elongation of shoots which, in turn, produces

Fig. 4. Typical life forms of high-mountain plants
A — prostrate shrub (e.g. *Salix reticulata)*   B — cushion plants (e.g. *Androsace helvetica)*

dwarfing. Furthermore, the various plant organs are frequently damaged, the terminal shoots broken and the leaves and flowers tattered. In the uneven topography of the mountains the direction of the winds changes constantly. Air currents are influenced not only by the configuration of the relief but also by the temperature differences in the valleys, the ridges and on the different facing slopes. Sometimes the situation is so complex that measurements by normal meteorological methods are practically impossible. In such cases information as to the direction of the prevailing ground winds may have to be gleaned from the forms of the local vegetation. The wind-trained tree, where wind pressure bends the branches to a point permanently in a leeward direction, is a striking example. There is also the so-called 'snow abrasion' and the coat of frozen snow and ice on the windward side of trunks and branches; only a minimum of buds are formed on this side. Wind also damages the wood-forming tissues inside the trunk and branches; these develop much better on the leeward side and so result in an asymmetrical ring formation. In very windy places the growth rings are dense and narrow, the wood hard and heavy, and often very resinous. The most wind-trained of trees must include the spruce, mountain ash, beech, larch and some other species. It is thus possible to make a reliable map of the prevailing winds in the variegated topography of the mountains.

A special category of wind in larger mountains is the so-called 'foehn' wind. This is a warm, dry wind blowing down into the foothills. After crossing the mountains, it becomes 1°C warmer with every 100 m drop in altitude. The effect on vegetation is generally beneficial; in man, however, it often causes headaches and neurasthenia.

THE RELATIONSHIP BETWEEN
HIGH-MOUNTAIN AND LOWLAND PLANTS

A keen observer of nature will notice that many taxa growing in the warm lowlands have close relatives in the high mountains, differing only in a few characteristics. Closer investigation will show that they are related taxa, classified by botanists as separate, independent species or as lesser categories such as races, varieties, and the like.

By way of example, compare two species of the genus *Epilobium* growing on alluvial river gravel. *Epilobium dodonaei* has a wide distribution range extending from the foothills of the French Alps to the Carpathians, south as far as Sicily and across the Balkans and Asia Minor to Armenia and the Caucasus. Within this vast range it naturally exhibits marked variations. It is mostly found in foothill localities but it can occur in mountains and sometimes even at subalpine levels. Sometime at the end of the glacial period, certain populations of this species in the western Alps became adapted to the very different high-mountain conditions, so that today it has diverged so far as to be classified as a distinct species *Epilobium fleischeri*. Besides growing at altitudes above 1,000 m, even as high as 2,700 m, it differs from the ancestral species by its low, sometimes even prostrate habit; it is never more than 40 cm in height, whereas *E. dodonaei* with its much shorter and broader leaves and larger flowers grows to a height of more than 100 cm. Even more striking is a comparison of the indumentum (hair covering) with *E. dodonaei* specimens from the warm and dry regions of Asia Minor. Here *E. dodonaei* var. *canescens* is distinguished from the glabrous *E. fleischeri* by its dense, hairy stems and foliage.

Of course, such differences are not always so striking or so permanent as to enable a clear distinction between the two taxa. In many cases the change of morphological and biological characters is gradual and is correlated with the gradual change from the lowland to the montane climate. A distinction between the two extremes is often impossible and usually depends on the subjective view of the individual botanist.

Other striking examples of lowland and high-mountain pairs are the blue fleabanes *(Erigeron acer* ssp. *acer* and *E. acer* ssp. *angulosus)*, the kidney-vetches *(Anthyllis vulneraria* ssp. *vulneraria* and *A. vulneraria* ssp. *alpestris)*, the sorrels *(Rumex acetosa* and *R. arifolius)*, the wood forget-me-not *(Myosotis sylvatica* and *M. alpestris)*, the basil thyme *(Acinos arvensis* and *A. alpina)*, which all exhibit their own characteristics. In the mountain species the leaves are generally thicker and less divided, the epidermal cells being thick-walled. In addition they have fewer flowers, more compact flower heads and larger seeds.

The formation of such species as a result of environmental influences is found only in a small number of families and genera. These are mostly groups which are young and recent from an evolutionary point of view.

Sometimes, over periods covering thousands or even tens or hundreds of thousands of years, closely related montane taxa eventually became separated and isolated; they come to evolve along divergent lines and these result in the development of marked morphological differences. Closely related species occupying mutually exclusive areas are called vicariants.

One of the principal barriers to the spread and overlap of species from open habitats was the spread of uninterrupted forest up to mountain level in the post-glacial period. This isolated the species of non-forested habitats of the lowlands from those above the upper timber line at alpine level. This natural process has been disrupted to a considerable extent by man with his intensive cultivation of the land, clearing of forests and transformation of mountain slopes into pastures and fields. Thus certain thermophilous lowland species were able to make their way high up into the mountains, particularly on the southern slopes. As a contrary move, certain mountain species began their descent into the valleys and foothills. Before man's interference, only water courses and avalanches made possible such descents and migrations of mountain species. Disruption of the natural barrier has therefore made it possible for species to interbreed and so to produce hybrids, some of which have a greater vitality than their parent plants with the consequence of being able to spread over a wider area. As examples of this last development, the now common and widespread sweet vernal grass *(Anthoxanthum odoratum)* is considered to be a hybrid between the lowland species *A. ovatum* and the alpine species *A. alpinum.* Similarly *Helianthemum nummularium* ssp. *obscurum,* annual meadow-grass *(Poa annua),* bird's foot trefoil *(Lotus corniculatus)* and other common species are probably the result of a similar process.

The differences between mountain and lowland plants have long attracted the interest of botanists, who have tried to

Fig. 5. Form of a lowland plant (A) after being transplanted to a mountain habitat (B) according to G. Bonnier's experiments with the common dandelion *(Taraxacum officinale)* and ox-eye daisy *(Leucanthemum vulgare)*

determine to what extent alpine characters are hereditary or merely due to environmental influence. A noted experimenter in this field was the French botanist G. Bonnier who in the late 19th century transplanted many species, which had been multiplied by vegetative means (i.e. to obtain genetically uniform material), at various elevations in the Alps and Pyrenees as well as in Paris. Lowland plants grown under high-mountain conditions up to 2,400 m above sea level were dwarfed, their leaves were thicker and a darker green in colour and their flowers were larger. They exhibited variation in structure, and plants which were annuals often became perennial. Only after many years did Bonnier deduce from this work that lowland species or races may only differ from high alpine species as a result of environmental influences. For example, *Juniperus communis* and *J. communis* ssp. *nana* are genetically very similar and also *Acinos arvensis* and *A. alpina*. Similar opinions to those of Bonnier were voiced in the early 20th century by F. E. Clements of the United States on the basis of his experiments in Colorado and California. He too confirmed that lowland species take on the appearance of alpine species when transplanted to a mountain environment. Similar conclusions reached by other botanists who had performed numerous similar experiments, involving the transplanting of lowland plants to the high mountains and vice versa, showed yet again that these changes are for the most part environmentally induced, and not genetically fixed; when the plants are transferred back to their original habitats or their seeds sown in the lowland habitats they usually revert to their original form.

Scientists who have studied the problem and performed such experiments include A. Kerner of Vienna, C. Nägeli of Munich, J. D. Clausen, D. D. Keck and W. M. Hiesey of California, and G. Turesson of Sweden.

FROM MOUNTAIN FORESTS
TO PERMANENT SNOW

The visitor to the mountains can see, almost in a matter of hours, a variety of plant communities, which would normally require a journey of several thousand kilometres say from the Mediterranean region across the whole of central Europe and Scandinavia to the Arctic Circle and beyond. That is how rapidly and markedly the climate and vegetation changes as one climbs from the foothills to the highest peaks. The effects of soil and climate on vegetation were first clearly formulated by Alexander Humboldt, who on his travels through South and Central America in the years 1799—1805, acquired a mass of knowledge contributing to his theories on the horizontal and vertical zonation of vegetation.

By the late 19th century the altitudinal division of vegetation had already been worked out in some detail for the Alps. Since then many scientists have come up with various revisions more or less differing from one another. Let us take a look at the basic and generally accepted vertical pattern of distribution. The Alps constitute a very extensive range with conditions differing markedly in the northern, central and southern parts. The northern margins are influenced by the oceanic climate with a rainfall as high as 3,000 mm per year. In the central Alps the climate tends to be continental in character with fairly low precipitation, as little as 400 mm in some valleys with great differences between summer and winter temperatures. On the southern margins rainfall is again higher because the mountains catch the rain from the Mediterranean; the annual temperature, however, is higher than on the northern margins.

The northern chain of the Alps may roughly be divided, as with the other mountains of central Europe, into distinguishing altitudinal belts: the colline or hill belt with its predominating oak forest, the submontane (according to some authorities the mountain) belt with beech forest predominating, the mountain (according to some authorities the oreal) belt with spruce forest, the subalpine belt with spread of dwarf pine or other shrubs (e.g. *Alnus viridis, Rhododendron*), the alpine belt with herbaceous perennials and low shrubs, the transitional subsnowline belt, and finally the snow belt — the region of permanent snow. This basic division is applicable to most mountain ranges: the mountain belt still has forests, the sub-alpine belt merely has shrubs and solitary trees, while the alpine belt with its harsh, high-mountain climate denies the growth of trees or even the larger shrubs. In the central Alps the make-up of plant communities and species composition differs at the various levels. At the lower, non-forested levels there will be vegetation like that of the steppe — xerophilous and thermophilous plants, followed by forests of pine, spruce, larch and cembra pine. In the southern chain of the Alps the forests are of the thermophilous oak *Quercus pubescens,* Spa-nish chestnut *(Castanea sativa)* and, at a higher level still, the beech *(Fagus sylvatica).* The upper limit of these altitudinal belts in the Alps is approximately as follows: colline or hill belt — between 550 and 1,000 m above sea level, submontane belt — between 800 and 1,700 m, mountain belt — between 1,700 and 2,400 m, subalpine belt — between 2,200 and 2,400 m, alpine belt — between 2,600 and 2,800 m, snow belt — between 2,500 and 3,200 m above sea level.

If we make a comparison with other mountain ranges we see that the vertical distribution of vegetation is only a rough classification; it depends on a wide range of factors. For ex-ample, in the High Tatras in Czechoslovakia, with a maxi-mum height of 2,663 m, the order of the altitudinal belts is as follows: colline or hill belt — up to 700 m, submontane belt — up to 1,250 m, mountain belt — up to 1,550 m, subalpine belt — up to 1,800 m, alpine belt — up to 2,300 m, subnival belt — above 2,300 m.

In Bulgaria, the Rila Mountains with a maximum altitude of 2,925 m above sea level, have thermophilous oak forest up to 1,000 m (in the colline or hill belt), beech forest with fir in the submontane belt up to 1,600 m and Macedonian pine forest *(Pinus peuce)* and spruce predominating up to 2,000 m in the mountain belt, then up to about 2,500 m comes the subalpine belt with dwarf pine with, at the highest elevations, alpine grasslands. Similar vertical distribution will be found in many other mountain ranges, chiefly in the temperate zone of the northern hemisphere and within reach of moist oceanic climates. It is understandable that the mountain chains of central Asia, with their marked continental climate, have a very different vertical distribution from that of Scandinavian mountains or of the Alps, Carpathians, Pyrenees and Cordilleras. There is no uniform pattern which can apply equally to all high-mountain chains.

One of the most striking phenomena of high-mountain vegetation is the upper forest limit or timber line. This separates two basic units of higher mountains — the mountain forest region and the unforested alpine region. The trees which constitute the timber line differ in the various mountain ranges. In the Vosges, with their oceanic climate, the line is formed by beech; in the northern Alps with a climate tending to be oceanic the spruce forms the line; in the central Alps, with their continental climate, by larch and cembra pine, in the High Tatras mainly by spruce (sometimes together with cembra pine); and in the North American Cordilleras by entirely different trees such as rough-branched Mexican pine *(Pinus montezumae)* or white-bark pine *(Pinus albicaulis)*, Rocky Mountain fir *(Abies lasiocarpa)* and mountain hemlock *(Tsuga mertensiana)*. In the Himalayas the line is formed by Himalayan fir *(Abies spectabilis)*, Himalayan yew *(Taxus wallichiana)* and *Sorbus tianshanica* while in the Tien Shan mountains of central Asia it is formed by the common walnut *(Juglans regia)*, the maple *(Acer turkestanicum)* and the apple *(Malus kirghisorum)*.

Not only are there differences in the species of trees growing at the upper forest limit of the various mountain ranges but there are also variations in the altitude of the timber-line. In the Alps this is generally located at 1,950 m above sea level; its lowest point is at 1,530 m above sea level in the region of Santis in the northern limestone Alps with its highest point at

2,330 m in Wallis. In the southern Carpathians in Rumania it
is located at a height of 1,850 m above sea level, while in the
Altai the forest extends to 2,000 or 2,400 m, in the Hindu
Kush to 3,000 or 3,500 m, in the Pamirs to 3,000 m, in the
Himalayas to 2,400 or 4,700 m, and in the Cordilleras up to
3,600 m. In the Cordilleras, which run north to south in the
western part of North America, this limit has, however, a descending trend in a northward direction until, in Alaska, it is
not more than 500 to 600 m above sea level. A similarly low
timber line is to be found in Tierra del Fuego at the southern
tip of South America and similarly at Kamchatka in Asia
where it is no more than 300 m above sea level. Thus the
timber line tends to drop towards the polar regions and towards the oceans. This phenomenon can also be observed in
the vertical distribution of a given tree species as, for example,
in the case of the beech *Fagus sylvatica.* In southern Sweden,
Denmark, northern Germany and northern Poland it forms
magnificent displays at the coastline; in the mountains of
central Europe it grows from 300 m to 600 m above sea level;
in Albania in the Balkan Peninsula from 1,200 m upwards;

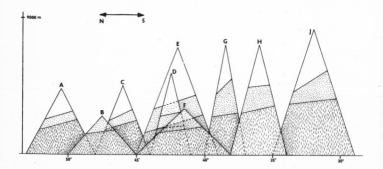

Fig. 6. Comparison of the maximum levels of the snow line and upper
timber line in some mountain ranges of Eurasia according to latitude.
White — areas of permanent snow and ice above the snow line. Dotted —
alpine areas between the upper timber line and snow line. Vertical shading
— forested areas.   A — Altai   B — Carpathians   C — Alps   D — Caucasus   E — Tien Shan   F — Apennines   G — Pamir   H — Hindu Kush
J — Himalayas

and at the southernmost margin of its range, on Mount Etna in Sicily, it is as high up as 2,000 m.

As already stated the temperature of the air decreases with increasing elevation and in consequence the growing season becomes shorter. The growth of trees is affected by any such adverse conditions because they are not protected by a snow cover in winter and are thus incapable of developing normally at certain altitudes. At higher altitudes they appear only in dwarf form and the point is reached at even greater heights when they are unable to germinate at all. In the Alps, for example, the average temperature of the air at the upper forest limit in July is 8.4° to 12.4° C, although in some places single trees can grow in a range of 7.8 — 10.8° C. Apart from temperature, the location of the upper timber line is determined also by the accumulation of snow and the duration of the snow cover in winter, the presence of strong winds, and the size of the mass and height of the mountain range.

Mention has already been made of the fact that solitary trees may grow amid dwarf pines as much as 200 to 300 m above the upper forest limit in the subalpine belt. The line joining the trees growing at least 5 m tall is called the tree line. Above this limit there are only dwarf and greatly deformed trees. In the belt between this line and the actual upper forest limit it is a struggle for survival at the limits of existence on the part of the various tree species.

As a rule, the upper forest limit does not follow a straight course over a long distance; it is irregular, up in one place and down in another. The more uneven the topography, the more complex are the temperature, wind, soil and other conditions. Forest is entirely lacking on steep rock faces and where avalanches occur regularly there will be a long tongue of unforested soil reaching far down into the valley.

A natural lowering of the timber line also occurs in the cirques, i.e., in circular, deep recesses cut into the mountainsides which are confined by steep walls, with screes and moraines. These were originally hollowed out by avalanches, firn and glaciers during the glacial periods, and by water erosion and disintegration through frost. Of all the montane habitats these cirques with their diverse climatic and soil conditions are usually the richest in plant and animal life on the mountain ridges. An important factor in the development of cirques and the preservation of their specific flora is the anemo-orographic system — a special combination of orographic and climatic conditions occurring where elongated valleys are oriented in the direction of the prevailing winds. In such valleys the air stream gains speed and after surmounting the summit falls into the leeward turbulent space of the cirque. In winter snow forms huge cornices on the upper edge of the cirque. Later these fall down the steep rock walls and become one of the chief obstacles to the spread of forest.

The natural upper forest limit has also been dramatically changed by centuries of human interference, for example through the burning of forest land, the spread of mountain pastures and the felling of mountain trees for their high-quality timber. In mountains long inhabited by man the forest limit has been lowered by about 200 m to 300 m. The course of such changes can best be seen in mountain ranges which have been little affected as yet. For instance, in uninhabited parts of the Andes and in New Zealand, *Nothofagus* species form a compact timber line, broken only in the vicinity of human habitations. The same is true in the Himalayas, where there are still compact stands of *Picea morinda, Abies webbiana* and other trees at the upper forest limit. In some cases the composition of herbaceous plants and shrubs above the present timber line is a reminder of the extent of the original forest growth. In the Alps, for example, the mezereon *(Daphne mezereum)*, the elder *(Sambucus racemosa)*, the alpine rose *(Rosa pendulina)*, wood rush *(Luzula luzulina)*, *Homogyne alpina*, whorled Solomon's seal *(Polygonatum verticillatum)*, hard fern *(Blechnum spicant)* and other species are typical members of such a zone.

STRUGGLE FOR SURVIVAL

The briefest of glances at a giant mountain with its snow-covered peak tells us much about the different climatic conditions at various altitudes on its slopes. In summer, when vegetation is lush at the base, with fruits ripening on many plants and early species nearing the end of their life cycle, plants at a higher elevation are just beginning to wake up while higher still there lies the realm of permanent snow and ice.

Most striking is the decrease in temperature with increasing altitude. On average it drops 0.5° to 0.6°C every 100 m in altitude. The decrease, however, may be smaller or greater or even irregular, depending on many other factors such as distance from the ocean to the interior, the height of the mountain range, the season of the year and even the position of a slope. The temperature gradient also differs at various elevations. In mountainous topography it may even happen that at lower elevations in a valley the temperature is lower than on the surrounding ridges, a phenomenon known as temperature inversion.

Precipitation is another factor which varies greatly in the mountains, increasing with altitude. On the windward side of a mountain the ascending air currents are cooled, water vapour gradually condenses and then falls in the form of rain and snow. On the leeward side the descending air currents are warmed and can retain increasing amounts of water vapour so that such areas are usually dry and, if facing south, southwest or southeast, also warm. This is the main reason for the large proportion of xerophilous and thermophilous plant species on that side. Not only are there differences in the quantity of rainfall but also in the number of rainy days; for example on the northern side of the Alps the amount is roughly twice that on the southern side. Rainfall, of course, does not increase indefinitely with increasing elevation. It does so only up to a certain altitude above sea level, which is called the belt of maximum precipitation. Beyond this it again decreases. Only in a few instances does precipitation reach its maximum at the summit. In the Alps, for example, in the Mont Blanc massif, where the highest peak is 4,807 m, besides vertical precipitation, i.e. rain and snow, horizontal precipitation is also very important for mountain vegetation, for example, frequent fogs blown by winds and caught in the crowns of the forest.

Of foremost importance for alpine plants, however, is the snow cover. Its depth as well as its duration are determining factors in the formation of the variegated mosaic of plant communities. Plants which grow in places exposed to strong winds, but practically without any snow, include the three-leaved rush *(Juncus trifidus)*, some species of sedge *(Carex)* and fescue-grass *(Festuca)*, *Loiseleuria procumbens*, mountain avens *(Dryas octopetala)*, and in the arctic regions *Diapensia lapponica*, lichens such as *Alectoria ochroleuca*, *Thamnolia vermicularis* and others. Plants growing around the valley snow patches are quite different species and include *Salix herbacea*, *Arabis caerulea*, *Ranunculus pygmaeus*, *Soldanella pusilla*, *Saxifraga androsacea*, *Sagina saginoides* and *Sibbaldia procumbens*. Maps showing the distribution of various plant communities have much in common with maps showing the persistence of the snow cover. Because the temperature under a thick cover of snow is fairly constant, dropping only slightly below 0° C, even plants which are sensitive to frost and which would otherwise be killed by the harsh mountain climate are able to survive under that cover. They are protected not only against low temperatures but also against the drying influence of strong winds. That is why so many plants at the alpine level survive the winter with evergreen leaves and, with the light penetrating through the snow, can even commence photosynthetic activity and the growth of new leaves.

Another line of importance in the high mountains is the snow line. The climatic snow line is that above which the snow never melts. Only rarely are flowering plants found above this line and then mostly on nunataks — isolated snowless rock masses. Mostly to be found there are certain microscopic sporiferous plants, chiefly algae, lower fungi and lichens. Some find their way there by chance usually from lower elevations while others grow there permanently. Some algae and lower fungi known only to occur on these areas of permanent ice and snow are called cryophytes. Many species of these organisms have been found throughout the world, on glaciers from Greenland to the Himalayas, in the Cordilleras and in the Antarctic. The cells of many of them contain pigments which appear to serve as a protection against strong ultraviolet radiation. When these organisms multiply, particularly in summer, the snow fields and glaciers are coloured in various shades of green and red. Such blood-coloured snow used to bring terror to the hearts of simple mountain folk who believed them to be the foreboding of some misfortune. Their superstitious beliefs were often proved right, for in the high mountains with their avalanches, gales and sudden melting of snow there is no dearth of calamities.

The snow line occurs at various elevations in high mountain chains and is dependent on many factors. In the Alps it is 2,500 to 3,350 m above sea level and 700 to 1,000 m above the timber line, in the Caucasus it is 2,700 to 3,000 m and in the Cordilleras in the United States 2,800 to 4,000 m above sea level. It is highest in western Tibet and the northern part of the Andes in Chile and Argentina — almost 6,500 m above sea level.

SOIL IN THE HIGH MOUNTAINS

Soil as we know it in the fertile lowlands is not to be found in high mountains. There, fragments of rock from the peaks and steep rocky slopes become dislodged and hurtle down, accumulating at the base in the form of screes and stone fields.

Physical, not chemical weathering prevails here, and the biological effect of micro-organisms and lichens is negligible. Only on older debris, in the valley bottoms or on plateaux does soil begin to form. Low temperatures and heavy moisture cause excessive washing of the soil and continual depletion of nutrients. The first pioneer plants leave behind organic matter when they die but this does not have time to decompose so that acidic raw humus accumulates.

The deeper soil which develops on siliceous rock is called ranker, that which forms on basic rock is called rendzina. On basic rock, however, the effect of acidic humus only rarely prevails over the alkaline character of the underlying rock. In high mountains, where rocks for the most part rise above the surface, the difference between acidic rocks with a high percentage of quartz and silicates (e.g. granite, gneiss and mica schist) and basic rocks with a low percentage of silicone compounds but a high percentage of calcium and magnesium carbonate (e.g. limestone and dolomite) is reflected in the composition of the vegetation. Between the two extremes, there are the so-called neutral rocks such as basalt, amphibolite, porphyry, phyllite, and andesite, which contain feldspars rich in sodium and calcium and which yield soil of medium fertility.

Many plant species grow solely on limestone or dolomite (calcicoles), others solely on siliceous rocks (calcifuges). A large group of plants which sometimes form whole plant communities grow only on a specific type of rock and are to be found only very occasionally on other types of rock. Yet another group is formed by plants without any special rock requirements. Knowledge of these requirements is very important, for example, for the rock-garden grower, so that his efforts to cultivate certain types of plants do not meet with failure.

High-mountain plants that grow   a)   on basic rocks

Androsace helvetica,   Arabis alpina,   Carex firma,   C. tatrorum,   Doronicum grandiflorum,   Draba tomentosa,   Dryas octopetala,   Festuca versicolor,   Gentiana clusii,   Petrocallis pyrenaica,   Poa alpina,   Potentilla caulescens,   Primula auricula, Ranunculus parnassifolius,   Rhododendron hirsutum,   Saxifraga biflora,   Sedum atratum,   Sesleria varia,   Thlaspi rotundifolium.

b)   on acidic siliceous rocks

Achillea moschata,   Campanula barbata,   Carex curvula,   Doronicum clusii,   Eritrichium nanum,   Festuca vivipara,   Gentiana   acaulis,   Juncus   trifidus,   Phyteuma   hemisphaericum,   Potentilla aurea,   Primula hirsuta,   Rhododendron ferrugineum,   Salix   herbacea,   Saussurea   alpina,   Saxifraga bryoides,   S. cotyledon,   S. exarata,   Vaccinium myrtillus,   V. vitis-idaea.

More fertile soil is found beside mountain streams, where there may be meadows of tall herbaceous plants on which chamoix, ibexes and other animals feed and further enrich the soil with their nitrogenous waste products. Large quantities of nitrogenous substances accumulate in the vicinity of shepherds' huts where sheep or cattle congregate. One of the principal plants found growing in such places is the tall sorrel *Rumex alpinus.* Large masses of this species will indicate human habitation even when mountain huts have not been used for years.

It may sometimes happen that one will find calcicole plants in a granite region or calcifuges among limestone. Closer investigation, however, often reveals that the material from which the soil developed is not derived from the local rock but was transported there by a glacier, water or avalanche from a distance of several kilometres.

THE SPREAD
OF HIGH-MOUNTAIN PLANTS

Many plant species become established on inaccessible mountain peaks where they may even flower and bear fruit. How
did they get there? In most cases they were transported there
by the wind, which picked up the spores, seeds and fruits in
the valleys and on mountain slopes. Sometimes whole clumps
may have been torn away and carried to new places, often
many kilometres away or several hundred metres higher up.
If the plants find conditions in the new habitat even slightly
congenial they will begin to grow. This is a common feature
with algae, lichens and mosses, but many flowering plants
will grow in a rock crevice. Sometimes the wind blows whole
plants over fields of firm snow, e.g. clumps of houseleeks
(Sempervivum), cushions of *Saxifraga* or tufts of the round-
leaved penny cress *(Thlaspi rotundifolium)*.

Few high-mountain plants are spread by animals, chiefly
because these become rarer with increasing altitude. An important role is played by birds which sometimes carry seeds to
inaccessible peaks. Birds usually feed on fleshy fruits and
solitary specimens of plants producing such fruits may be
found on bare rock even above the snow line. As a rule, however, they do not bear further fruit at such altitudes. Examples
of such plants found at the snow line include the common
cotoneaster *(Cotoneaster integerrimus)*, the dwarf juniper *(Juniperus communis* ssp. *nana)*, *Vaccinium myrtillus*, the arctic
bearberry *(Arctostaphylos uva-ursi)*, crowberry *(Empetrum ni-
grum* ssp. *hermaphroditum)*, *Rosa pendulina* and *Ribes petraeum*. Naturally, birds also disseminate plants with dry
fruits in their faeces or feathers; examples here include the
alpine plantain *(Plantago alpina)*, the milk-vetch *(Astragalus
frigidus)*, *Geum montanum* and others. The Nutcracker, a bird
the size of a jay inhabiting the deep coniferous woods of the
mountains, is a specialist in distributing the cembra pine *(Pi-*

nus cembra) above the upper forest limit. It is fond of eating the seeds of this pine, but because it is in the habit of storing food and hiding the seeds for future use, it sometimes happens that seeds are overlooked and these germinate in due course.

Water either in the form of rain or melting snow is obviously instrumental in spreading montane plants to lower levels. At best, seeds will catch a foothold and germinate a short distance down stream; or in the foothills on alluvial gravel. Otherwise, if washed further down into rivers they will generally be irretrievably lost.

Man is one of the principal agents by which fruits and seeds may be distributed. On his expeditions into the mountains he may carry with him plants from lower elevations or weeds which either may gain a temporary foothold or become established permanently.

HIGH-MOUNTAIN PLANTS
IN THE LOWLANDS

Sometimes typical alpine plants may be found even at low elevations, particularly near water courses serving as a means of transport. Generally alpine plants which grow on rubble and rocks find congenial conditions on stone and gravel alluvial deposits. There they are able to gain a foothold because, being adapted to a brief growing season, they can flower and sometimes even bear fruit before these alluvial deposits are flooded or dried out. Most alpines require a great deal of light and water so that unshaded situations supplied with percolating water are very suitable. In the Alps and Carpathians these are mostly the alpine toadflax *(Linaria alpina)*, *Gypsophila repens*, *Arabis alpina*, *Hutchinsia alpina*, *Campanula cochleariifolia*, *Kernera saxatilis*, alpine meadow grass *(Poa alpina)*, yellow mountain saxifrage *(Saxifraga aizoides)* and *Tolpis staticifolia*. These species are carried many kilometres below the timber line by some alpine rivers.

Riverside meadows and clearings in riverside forests are other lowland habitats where plants of tall alpine meadows become established. Species to be found here are *Veratrum album*, *Adenostyles alliariae*, leopard's bane *(Doronicum austriacum)*, *Gentiana asclepiadea*, the alpine willow-herb *(Epilobium alpestre)*, *Cicerbita alpina*, the crowfoot *(Ranunculus platanifolius)*, *Rumex alpinus*, monkshood *(Aconitum napellus)* and *Viola biflora*.

Rivers and streams, of course, are not the only means whereby alpine plants make their way to lower elevations. They may also be carried there by the wind or by avalanches and sometimes, in the case of plants growing in rock crevices, by boulders falling into valleys from heights of several hundred metres. Alpine taxa which have made their way to the lowlands or hill country are called dealpines. If they continue to have some sort of link with their original habitat at alpine level they are termed syndealpines; if they occur as isolated instances at lowland elevations they are termed apodealpines. Apodealpines are generally relicts, i.e. species which have survived from the glacial period when they were common in the lowlands and which, after the retreat of the ice sheet, remained in congenial places such as cool, deep ravines and narrow river canyons. Examples of such relicts in central Europe are dwarf birch *(Betula nana)*, *Pedicularis sceptrum-carolinum*, *Primula auricula* and *Saxifraga paniculata*.

HIGH-MOUNTAIN PLANTS
ABOVE THE SNOW LINE

It has been mentioned already that one will find many species of lichens (e.g. genera *Rhizocarpon, Lecidea, Umbilicaria),* algae, and other spore-bearing plants above the snow line. But what about flowering plants? And to what height do they make their way?

The snow zone does not mean merely snow and ice. Bare rocks are to be found there too, and in some places the snow may melt in exceptionally warm years. Some species find their way there from below the snow line by natural means, and are being discovered by mountaineering expeditions made by naturalists. There are no vascular plants growing in the snow zone which cannot be found at alpine levels.

In the Alps, the most thoroughly investigated of the mountain ranges, the highest growing flowering plant discovered to date is *Ranunculus glacialis,* found on Finsteraarhorn at 4,275 m above sea level. Other species growing at elevations above 4,000 m in the Alps are *Androsace alpina, Saxifraga muscoides, S. biflora, S. bryoides, S. moschata, Gentiana brachyphylla, Draba fladnizensis,* alpine meadow grass *(Poa alpina),* alpine toadflax *(Linaria alpina), Phyteuma globulariifolium* ssp. *pedemontanum* and *Achillea atrata.* The highest recorded dicotyledonous annual to date is *Euphrasia minima,* found growing at an altitude of 3,500 m above sea level. On Gerlach, the highest peak (2,663 m) of the High Tatra Mountains, species of seed plants have been found, among them *Primula minima, Gentiana frigida, Saxifraga bryoides,* wavy meadow grass *(Poa laxa)* and *Oreochloa disticha.*

Record heights are naturally to be looked for in the highest mountain range of all, the Himalayas. In areas investigated so far certain seed plants were found at elevations above 6,000 m, e.g. members of the genus *Poa* and *Carex,* three species of *Leontopodium* and several species of *Saussurea.* The world's highest-growing plants, found in Kashmir, are *Ermania koelzii* of the family *Brassicaceae* found at a height of about 6,300 m and *Arenaria musciformis* of the family *Caryophyllaceae* found at a height of 6,218 m. The highest recorded tree is *Polylepis* of the family *Rosaceae* growing in the Andes up to heights of about 5,000 m.

DISTRIBUTION
OF HIGH-MOUNTAIN PLANTS

The distribution of individual high-mountain plant species is greatly influenced by ecological factors, primarily climate and soil. Each different species of plant has its own particular distribution or range. Comparison, however, shows that the areas occupied by certain species have several general characteristics. Areas are accordingly divided into several different types. Some of these will be described briefly in the following text. First, however, it is necessary to realize that the influence of the environment as it exists today is not the only factor determining the distribution pattern. We must go far back into the past often tens or even hundreds of thousands of years, to find out about the great changes in the Earth's climate and the evolution of new species. This is the key to understanding what today is often an extremely complex area structure as well as great diversity within individual taxa.

The main differentiation of present-day taxa and the complex area structure were predominantly influenced by the glacial and interglacial periods in the Quaternary epoch or, in other words, during the past million years. The Pleistocene glaciation, which in four stages primarily affected a great part of Eurasia and North America, brought about the extinction of many species and with many others a retreat from their original range. Plants which had been pushed from the north and from the mountains to lower altitudes mingled together and formed new plant communities. When the ice sheet receded, plants followed in its wake but now the structure of the vegetation was entirely different. That is how species originally alpine made their way to Scandinavia, and species originally arctic to the Alps, Carpathians and Caucasus. The warm interglacial and cold glacial periods caused the breakup of the once uninterrupted distribution areas of some species between the Pyrenees and eastern Asia. Further long evolution in iso-

lated parts of the range caused Europe's mountains to develop taxa differing from those which had remained in the
mountains of Central Asia and the Far East. Conditions in
Eurasia were more complex than those in North America in
that its mountain chains are mostly positioned east to west,
not north to south. They thus served as a barrier to the unim-
peded retreat and return of plant species in the wake of the
ice sheet; in North America, on the other hand, the mountains
posed no such obstacle.

These migrations of species as well as whole plant communities left behind them plants now known as relicts. These are
remnants of a once wide-spread population, living witnesses
of the past, species forced by changed climatic conditions to
enter congenial restricted locations, and remain there as sur-
vivors. For instance, in its southernmost locality in the Krko-
noše (Giant Mountains) in Czechoslovakia, *Rubus chamaemo-
rus,* a species widespread in northern Europe, occurs as a sur-
vivor of the glacial period when it grew in what was once the
tundra which covered most of central Europe. The same is

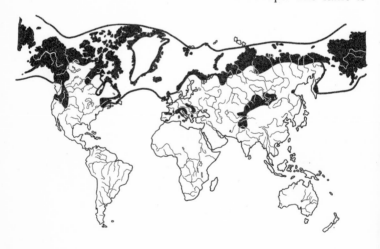

Fig. 7. Distribution of the circumpolar arctic-alpine species *Saxifraga oppositifolia*

true of other species, now common in the north, which grow as relicts in some of the peat-bogs of central Europe, e.g. the dwarf birch *(Betula nana)* and the downy willow *(Salix lapponum)*. Examples of very old relicts which have survived in the mountains of southern Europe from the warm Tertiary period are several species of the tropical family *Gesneriaceae* such as *Ramondia pyrenaica* in the Pyrenees and *Haberlea rhodopensis* in the Rhodope and Balkan mountains in Bulgaria.

Typical of the alpine flora of all high mountains in the world are the so-called endemic species, which, like relicts, have a very restricted range. Unlike the latter, however, they do not occur and have never occurred anywhere else. The high-mountain climate and diversity of the geological substrata as well as the topography are ideal for the evolution of endemic taxa. The larger and, above all, the more isolated a mountain range, the greater the number of endemics which evolve there. Some endemics may be quite old, their evolution dating from the Tertiary; these are called paleo-endemics. As a rule, they are comparatively isolated systematically and geographically from any of the nearest related taxa. Examples of

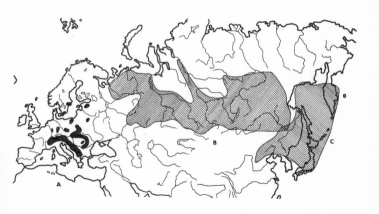

Fig. 8.   Distribution of the closely related species *Pleurospermum austriacum* (A), *P. uralense* (B) and *P. camtschaticum* (C)

paleo-endemics are *Daphne arbuscula* of the Muran High-lands in the Carpathians, whose closest relatives *D. striata* and *D. petraea* grow in the Alps, and *Delphinium oxysepalum* of the western Carpathians, whose closest relatives *D. dubium* and *D. montanum* grow in the southeastern and western Alps and in the Pyrenees respectively.

Far more numerous, however, are neo-endemic plants, taxa of recent formation, having evolved in the Quaternary epoch or even in the present epoch. More than two hundred of them have been found in the Alps alone, despite the fact that these

Fig. 9. Distribution of some high-mountain endemic plants in Eurasia
A — *Aquilegia pyrenaica* (Pyrenees and N. Spain) B — *Moehringia sedifolia* (formerly *M. dasyphylla*) (Maritime Alps) C — *Campanula pulla* (N. E. lime-stone Alps) D — *Androsace mathildae* (Apennines) E — *Campanula orea-dum* (Olympus) F — *Delphinium oxysepalum* (Western Carpathians) G — *Papaver lapponicum* (Arctic Norway and Russia) H — *Polemonium pulchellum* (northern Urals) J — *Draba scabra* (Caucasus) K — *Draba araratica* (Armenian Highlands) L — *Hyacinthus kopetdaghi* (Kopet Dagh) M — *Papaver croceum* (Mongolian Altai) N — *Callianthemum tibeticum* (Tibet) O — *Miyakea integrifolia* (Sakhalin) P — *Primula nipponica* (Japan).

mountains are of comparatively recent origin. They are mostly members of the genera *Primula, Saxifraga, Gentiana* and *Androsace*. Often neo-endemics cannot be considered as separate, individual species. Taxonomically they are usually lower units than species, and are usually classified as microspecies, subspecies or varieties. They develop in genera where certain traits and characters are easily changed by environmental influences. The genus *Hieracium* can serve as a good example. Twenty-three endemic species and races have been described in the Giant Mountains alone, and this is a small, central European range only 1,602 m high.

Examples of endemic species in various mountain ranges

ALPS — *Androsace brevis, Campanula alpestris, C. pulla, C. zoysii, Erigeron candidus, Gentianella engadinensis, Phyteuma sieberi, Primula allionii, P. clusiana, P. spectabilis, P. tyrolensis, Saxifraga vandellii, Soldanella minima*

PYRENEES — *Aquilegia pyrenaica, Lilium pyrenaicum, Petrocoptis pyrenaica, Ramonda myconi, Soldanella villosa*

APENNINES — *Androsace mathildae*

CARPATHIANS (entire range) — *Campanula carpatica, Erysium wittmannii, Festuca carpatica, Oxytropis carpatica, Poa granitica, Salix kitaibeliana*

WESTERN CARPATHIANS — *Cerastium arvense* ssp. *tatrae, Delphinium oxysepalum, Dianthus nitidus, Festuca tatrae, Pulsatilla halleri* ssp. *slavica, Saxifraga perdurans, Soldanella carpatica*

EASTERN CARPATHIANS — *Aquilegia nigricans, Chrysosplenium alpinum, Euphorbia carpatica, Phyteuma vagneri, Rumex carpaticus, Sesleria bielzii*

OLYMPUS — *Campanula oreadum, Rhynchosinapis nivalis*

SCANDINAVIA — *Draba cacuminum, Euphrasia lapponica, Primula scandinavica*

CAUCASUS — *Campanula ciliata, Delphinium caucasicum, D. dasycarpum, D. speciosum, Draba scabra, Gentiana caucasica, Lilium georgicum, Omphalodes rupestris, Poa caucasica, Ranunculus caucasicus*

ARMENIAN HIGHLANDS — *Draba araratica, Pedicularis araratica*

KOPET DAGH — *Hyacinthus kopetdaghi*

URALS — *Anemone uralensis, Cerastium krylovii, Epilobium uralense, Gypsophila uralensis, Linum boreale, Polemonium nudipedum, Rhodiola iremelica, Saussurea uralensis*

SAYAN and ALTAI — *Carex altaica, Papaver croceum, Pedicularis brachystachys, Veronica sajanensis*

TIBET — *Arenaria kausuensis, Callianthemum tibeticum, Corydalis tibetica, Cremanthodium humile, Omphalodes blepharolepis, Saussurea stella*

SAKHALIN — *Miyakea integrifolia*

HIGH MOUNTAINS OF JAPAN — *Artemisia sinanensis, Gentiana yakushimensis, Hieracium japonicum, Primula nipponica, Sanguisorba obtusa*

ROCKY MOUNTAINS — *Arenaria obtusiloba, Synthyris reniformis*

High-mountain plants have much in common with the plants of the arctic tundra and many species occur in both ecosystems. These are called arctic-alpine plants. Examples include the moss campion *(Silene acaulis)*, the three-leaved rush *(Juncus trifidus)*, the purple saxifrage *(Saxifraga oppositifolia)*, the mountain avens *(Dryas octopetala)*, the louse-wort *(Pedicularis verticillata)*, the reticulate willow *(Salix reticulata)*, *Lloydia serotina*, and *Hedysarum hedysaroides*. Some are found in the arctic regions of both hemispheres, others only in a certain small part. In addition, there are those species which grow only in the arctic tundra and are not to be found in more southerly mountain chains, e.g. *Cassiope hypnoides* and *C. tetragona, Carex lapponica, Ranunculus nivalis* and *Cerastium arcticum*. Despite many common aspects in the ecology of the tundra and high-mountain habitats, the two differ in many ways. Contrasting situations exist, for example, with respect to the soil. In the tundra the subsoil is permanently frozen (permafrost) because the summer is too brief for the ground to thaw out to a depth of more than several centimetres. In the high mountains there are much greater differences between day-time and night-time temperatures. Moreover, precipitation (except for the continental mountains of central Asia) is much higher even in winter, so that the thick covering of snow serves as an excellent protection for many less hardy plant species. Though the period of daylight in summer is shorter in the high mountains, the intensity of irradiation is much greater and also therefore the proportion of ultraviolet rays. Further, the diversity of the rock substrate and the resulting types of soil as well as the unevenness of the topography in the Alps are reasons why there are many more plant species than in the tundra. Mention has already been made of the great number of endemics; these comprise about a quarter of the total number of species in the Caucasus, the Balkan mountains and the Iberian Peninsula alone. However, the total number of species in the high mountain ranges is also uncommonly large — 4,000 in the Alps and some 6,000 in the Caucasus.

The alpine flora of the northern hemisphere consists primarily of herbaceous families. Unlike trees and shrubs whose woody stems live from year to year making them more prone to damage in winter, perennial herbaceous plants are far better equipped to survive the harsh, high-mountain conditions during this period as their aerial parts die back after each season's growth and their underground organs are protected.

The different alpine plant communities form a diverse and complex system. Species which grow in a limited mountain range and have also evolved there are designated as the floristic element of the given range; the species common to two or more mountain ranges form more general floristic elements. Others, over a lengthy period of evolution in isolated circumstances, have formed several species. This process is taking place continually.

Some mountain ranges, particularly in Asia, have not adequately been investigated as yet, not only from the viewpoint of plant systematics and the distribution of individual species, but also as regards their ecology. Such investigations will eventually yield much valuable knowledge.

PROTECTION AND PRESERVATION
OF THE ALPINE ENVIRONMENT

Almost 20 million square kilometres of the Earth's surface lie at heights of more than 2,000 m above sea level and it is often at these altitudes that nature is at her loveliest. Only man poses a threat to this unique world of the high mountains.

Man began to conquer the high mountains in times long past. As he believed them to be the home of the gods and feared the wrath of supernatural powers, he entered timidly at first. Later, he left his mark on the more accessible parts of some mountain ranges, changing them drastically. Eventually he burned forests and stands of dwarf pine, felled old trees, and put herds of cattle out to graze on the pastures thus created. Such action limited the output of certain springs and fouled the crystal-clear waters. The biological balance was disrupted. Erosion by wind and water has completed this work of destruction by removing the nourishing soil layer, exposing the underlying rock and drying out the springs. There are innumerable examples of such thoughtlessness on the part of man.

Man gradually began to settle in the mountains, to make his home there. In the mountains of Asia and South America there are settlements and monasteries at heights of 4,000 to 5,000 m above sea level; La Paz, the capital of Bolivia with its 350,000 inhabitants lies about 3,700 m above sea level. It is by no means difficult to get there, for planes land at the airport only a few hundred metres beyond the city. The railway in the Andes will take one higher — up to 4,880 m above sea level — and the roads rise even higher than that. The accessibility of the ore deposits makes mining an attractive proposition even at heights of more than 5,000 m, where man extracts silver, copper, tin, lead and other metals. In all of these ways, man slowly but surely encroaches upon the virgin wilderness of the high mountains. The danger is all the greater as the indirect effects of man's activity are also increasing rapidly day by day. Foremost of these is air pollution which is becoming a serious threat to the entire biosphere. Sulphur dioxide, benylpyrenes, ash, microscopic metal particles, radioactive chemicals and many other substances, chiefly gases from industrial plants, do great damage to plant and animal life. Some species which are particularly sensitive may even be exterminated. That is why, besides employing general preventive measures such as decreasing air pollution, it is necessary to focus attention on certain larger and as yet relatively untouched expanses of wilderness and to provide them with rigid protection. In most cases this is done through the establishment of national parks.

The first such park in the world was Yellowstone National Park in the Rocky Mountains, USA, opened in 1872. The years since then have seen the establishment of many more such parks for scientific, educational or recreational purposes in virgin or almost virgin territories. These include Mount McKinley National Park in Alaska, nearly 800,000 hectares in area, Waterton-Glacier International Peace Park in Canada and the United States (opened in 1932), Engadine National Park in the Swiss Alps (opened in 1914), Hohe Tauern National Park in Austria (opened in 1970), Gran Paradiso National Park, the first in Italy (opened in 1922), Del Valle de Ordesa o del Rio Ara National Park on the Spanish side of the Pyrenees (opened in 1918), Le Parc National des Pyrenees on the French side of the Pyrenees (opened in 1967), the Tatra National Park in the Carpathians (opened in 1948), and the 'Kavkazskii Zapovednik' in the Caucasus (opened in 1924). These are only a few of the many protected landscape areas in the world. Currently there are more than 20,000 such areas of various categories registered throughout the world ranging from small reserves to large national parks. Nowadays the establishment of national parks is coordinated on an international level, for they are unique territories of inestimable value to the science and culture of all mankind as giant laboratories in the wild. The population explosion and the vast expansion of industry, coupled with the increased exploitation of natural resources, make it necessary to protect more and more such territories. By doing so we are protecting nature not only against man but first and foremost for man himself and his future generations.

PLATES

Purple Spring Crocus
Crocus vernus HILL

Iridaceae

Before all the snow has melted and disappeared from the mountain meadows, they are already covered with drifts of these white-petalled flowers interspersed with pale to dark violet blossoms or white striped with violet. *Crocus vernus* is a typical early flowering spring plant of meadows and pastures in the Alps, Pyrenees, Corbières, Cevennes, Juras, Vosges, Schwarzwald, Apennines and mountains of the Balkan peninsula. It is noted for its wide vertical distribution, ranging from altitudes of 350 to 2,700 m above sea level in the Alps. It is the only member of the genus growing in large masses even above the alpine timber line.

Another similar crocus growing in the Alps is *C. biflorus*. It is found, however, only at the southern foot of these mountains, its range extending across Italy and the Balkans as far as the Middle East. The eastern Mediterranean region, particularly the Balkans and Asia Minor, is the evolutionary centre of the genus, which numbers some 80 species. *C. vernus* is the northernmost species and there are many and various cultivated species which have spread and become established in the wild throughout central Europe.

A noteworthy cultivar is the saffron *C. sativus*, which has been grown not for its ornamental value so much as for the orange-yellow pigment contained in the stigmas. This is used as food colouring and the dried stigmas as a spice.

Flowering period:
II — VI.
Perennial.
Height: 5 — 15 cm.
Corm:
With scaly skin which disintegrates into fibrous remains.
Leaves:
Narrow, linear.
Perianth segments:
6, joined to form a tube at the base; white or violet or white striped with violet.
Stamens: 3
Fruit: 3-part capsule.

Bulbocodium vernum L.

Syn. *Colchicum vernum* (L.) KER-GAWL.

Members of the lily family are often the loveliest of all mountain flowers, e.g. in the Alps *Lilium carniolicum, L. rubrum, L. bulbiferum, Fritillaria burnatii, Paradisia liliastrum, Asphodelus albus* and in the Pyrenees *Lilium pyrenaicum.* The illustrated species is one of these. The beauty of the violet-pink blossoms is particularly striking as they appear very early in spring, when the mountain meadows are still covered with melting snow. It is found in the Pyrenees, the southwestern Alps as far as Wallis and Aostatal, in a small area in Carinthia, in the Apennines, Serbia, southern Carpathians and in southern Russia. The species has a very wide vertical distribution, growing far above the timber line at altitudes of about 2,400 m above sea level as well as at lower elevations among thermophilous grasses.

Bulbocodium vernum is often classed in the genus *Colchicum,* which includes a great many species, most of them thermophilous, found mainly in the area extending from the eastern Mediterranean countries to India. Only two species — *Colchicum alpinum* and *C. autumnale* — grow in the Alps. Whereas colchicums flower in the autumn and the petals are joined to form a long tube, *Bulbocodium vernum* flowers in early spring and the petals are divided to the base. Both bulbocodiums and colchicums contain a highly poisonous alkaloid called colchicine.

Flowering period: II—III.
Perennial.
Height: 5—20 cm.
Corm: With brown to brown-black scales.
Leaves: Strap-shaped, up to 20 cm long, appear at the same time as the flowers.
Perianth segments: 6, pink or violet, up to 15 cm long, narrowing at the base.
Fruit: Capsule.

Bearberry

Arctostaphylos uva-ursi (L.) SPRENG.

Ericaceae

The genus *Arctostaphylos* contains some 70 species and is found only in the northern hemisphere. As with most members of the family *Ericaceae,* the leaves are leathery, evergreen and superbly adapted against drying out, invaluable especially in the case of those species in California. The genus traces its roots far back to the Tertiary period.

Bearberry is found in mountains and cooler regions as well as in lowlands throughout the northern hemisphere. A related species, *A. alpina,* has a similar range but it occurs farther north and higher in the mountains. Unlike bearberry, however, the leaves of this species are not persistent and the fruits are not scarlet but dark blue. Both species are spread by birds which feed on the fruit.

Bearberry forms spreading carpets in open, dry woods, and sometimes on stony pastures with alkaline to slightly acidic soils. In the Alps it is found up to elevations of 2,800 m. It contains the glycoside arbutin and tannins and was gathered as a drug-plant in England as early as the 13th century. Nowadays the dried leaves of this plant are widely used in the preparation of various medicines and medicinal teas, chiefly in the treatment of inflammation of the urinary passages. In the wild it may be mistaken for the cranberry; a good distinguishing feature is that the leaves of the latter are spotted brown on the underside.

Flowering period:
VI—IX.
Prostrate shrub.
Height:
20—40 cm.
Stem: Creeping, 30—100 cm long.
Leaves:
Leathery, evergreen, wedge-shaped obovate, entire.
Flower:
Bell-shaped with 5 recurved petal lobes, pink or white.
Fruit: Scarlet drupe.

1 — fruits

Spring Gentian

Gentiana verna L.

Gentianaceae

The genus *Gentiana* takes its name from the Illyrian king Gentio who, according to legends, was cured of a grave illness by the root of the gentian. Some species of this beautiful plant are still used for medicinal purposes to this day. Most important are the bitter glycosides gentiopicrin, gentiamarin, etc., found chiefly in the rhizomes and roots, which make the plant repellent to grazing cattle. *G. lutea, G. punctata, G. pannonica* and *G. purpurea,* for example, are collected for this purpose and even cultivated in countries where they are protected. They are used to make a number of medicines, particularly for the treatment of gastric disorders. In former days the yellow pigment gentisin obtained from the roots and rhizomes was used to dye cotton fabrics.

The spring gentian is the chief representative of some 15 species distributed throughout the mountains of Eurasia; these include *G. brachyphylla* and *G. bavarica.* The flowers of these species are almost cylindrical with lanceolate petal lobes whereas those of the low-growing gentians of the *G. acaulis* group are narrowly obconical with triangular petal lobes. Spring gentian grows in meadows, fens, pastures as well as on rocks, in both dry and damp localities, preferring soil with lime. Its range extends from the mountains of northern Spain across the Pyrenees, the mountains of central France, the Juras, Alps and alpine foothills to the Carpathians, Apennines and the Balkan mountains. In the north it is found in England and Ireland. In the Alps it grows up to and sometimes above 3,500 m.

Flowering period: III — VIII.
Perennial.
Height: 3 — 10 cm.
Rhizome: Slender.
Stem: Unbranched, single-flowered, square.
Leaves: In a ground rosette, lanceolate, pointed, up to 3 cm long, those on the flower stem in pairs (1 — 3).
Flower: Hypocrateriform, 5-petalled, dark azure blue, rarely white.

Saxifraga burseriana L.

The genus *Saxifraga* comprises some 370 species, most of which grow on rocks, screes and the like, as indicated by the scientific name derived from the Latin words *saxum,* meaning rock, and *frangere,* meaning to break. Often saxifrages are found even in tiny crevices in hard rock. Practically all are plants of the northern hemisphere, growing mostly in the temperate, boreal and arctic zones; North Africa's Atlas Mountains, the Yemen, Himalayas and Mexico mark their extreme southern limit. Only a few species are found in the southern hemisphere, in the Andes. Most species are adapted to life in a harsh climate, either in high mountains or in the far north. For example, *Saxifraga hirculus,* whose range embraces a great part of Eurasia and North America, occurs up to elevations of 5,600 m above sea level in the Himalayas; some species are found at even higher altitudes.

Its habit of growth makes *S. burseriana* ideally suited for harsh conditions. It is found in the northeastern and southeastern limestone and Dolomite Alps and in Jugoslavia, where it grows on rocks and screes, mostly at heights of 1,600 to 2,500 m above sea level. It is also sometimes found on the stone debris of Alpine rivers.

Flowering period: III — VII. Perennial.
Height: 3 — 7 cm.
Stems: Sturdy, forming dense, flat cushions together with leaves.
Leaves: Rigid, pointed, entire, spiny at the base, with dots of lime on the upper surface, grey-green.
Petals: 5, white, lined with red, 7 — 15 mm long.

Spring Anemone

Pulsatilla vernalis (L.) MILL.
Syn. *Anemone vernalis* L.

Ranunculaceae

Most of the 30 or so species of *Pulsatilla,* widespread throughout the northern hemisphere, are mountain or high-mountain plants. Their lovely flowers and their ornamental fruits with long silky hairs, facilitating dispersal by the wind, make them great favourites in the rock garden. European species include *P. vulgaris, P. montana, P. halleri, P. vernalis, P. alba* and *P. alpina. P. flavescens* is an example of an Asiatic species and *P. occidentalis* of the North American species.

Pulsatilla vernalis flowers as soon as the snow melts. Sometimes, when it is unusually warm, it will flower in winter in places where there is no snow, as the flower buds are formed in the previous autumn. As with all pulsatillas the plant is poisonous; it contains protoanemonin which, however, loses its toxic effect when the plant is dried.

P. vernalis grows on poor, acidic soils. In Europe its range extends from the Pyrenees across the Alps throughout central Europe to Scandinavia, as far as latitude 63° N. It is an old species which in the Quaternary period developed into various different types, depending on the habitat. The variety *alpestris* grows at higher elevations, chiefly on grassy and shrubby slopes at subalpine and alpine level, in the Alps as high as 3,600 m above sea level. The lowlands and hill country of central Europe, southern Sweden and Finland are the home of the variety *vernalis,* which grows mainly in pine stands and in heaths.

Flowering period:
IV—VII.
Perennial.
Height: 5—15 cm, when fruit develops up to 30 cm.
Leaves:
Long-petioled, laciniate.
Flowers:
Pendant at first, later upright.
Perianth segments:
6, violet and hairy outside, whitish inside,
15—35 mm long.
Fruit: Achene with hairy appendage up to 4 cm long.

Alpine Snowbell
Soldanella alpina L.

Primulaceae

Alpine meadows are a sight to behold when the snow melts. When warmed by the sun's rays, the blue-violet bell-shaped flowers of *Soldanella* will even begin to pierce through the thin crust of frozen snow. At subalpine and alpine elevations in the Alps it may be one of five species. At the highest level grows *S. pusilla* (up to 3,100 m), followed by *S. alpina* (up to 3,000 m), *S. austriaca* and *S. minima* (up to 2,500 m) and, in the wooded areas, *S. montana* (up to 1,700 m at the most).

S. alpina grows mainly in alpine meadows in places where snow stays a long time. It is also to be found on moist rocks, usually in basic, mostly calcareous soils but occasionally in neutral soils. It is found at elevations of 500 to 3,000 m in the Pyrenees, Auvergnes, Alps, Juras, Schwarzwald, Apennines and Illyrian mountains. The plants are adapted to a very short growing season, often less than three months, during which time they manage to grow, produce ripe seeds and form leaf and flower buds for the following year. This short cycle is made possible by the ability of the evergreen leaves to commence photosynthesis the moment the temperature rises above freezing point. *S. alpina* has some ten very closely related species, found mostly in the mountains of central and southern Europe.

Flowering period: IV—VII.
Perennial.
Height: 5—15 cm.
Leaves: Leathery, roundish reniform, entire.
Flowers: Funnel-shaped, 8—15 mm long, fringed, blue-violet, rarely white, in loose heads of 2 to 4.
Fruit: 10-toothed capsule, 10—15 mm long.

1—fruits

1

Purple Saxifrage
Saxifraga oppositifolia L.

Saxifragaceae

This is one of the commonest saxifrages found on both siliceous and calcareous soils. An arctic-alpine species, it grows throughout the northern parts of Eurasia from the British Isles across Scandinavia and the Kola Peninsula to northern Siberia, as well as in North America (mainly in Alaska), northern Canada and the United States (Wyoming and the Rocky Mountains), in Greenland and Iceland and in the mountains of central and southern Europe and central Asia. Latitude 83° 39′ N at the northern tip of Greenland marks the northernmost limit of its range. It is also one of the saxifrages growing at the highest elevations — in western Tibet as high as 6,000 m above sea level.

Saxifraga oppositifolia is a complex species which comprises numerous microspecies and subspecies, some with a very limited distribution. Such variety is not surprising for this group of plants existed in the northern hemisphere as early as the Ice Age. This is testified to by fossil finds of pollen, sometimes in places where the species no longer grows, e.g. in Holland and Denmark. Most widely distributed is ssp. *oppositifolia,* which grows up to 3,800 m above sea level in the Alps. A beautiful sight is the compact, ground-hugging ssp. *rudolphiana* of the eastern Alps and eastern Carpathians. Unusual is the location of the ssp. *amphibia,* endemic to the shores of Lake Constance, which are regularly flooded in summer; this subspecies is, however, probably already extinct.

Flowering period: IV—VIII.
Perennial.
Height: 1 — 5 cm.
Stem: Prostrate, spreading with numerous side shoots.
Leaves: Rigid, bristly on the margin, 2 — 8 mm long, blunt.
Sepals: Bristly, red.
Petals: 5, blunt or pointed, wine-red, later violet to blue, 5 — 15 mm long.

1 — leaves and flower

1

Bears-Ear
Primula auricula L.

This genus of immense size has been divided into many sections. One of these is the *Auricula* section whose members are typical alpine plants. Best known is *Primula auricula,* bearing yellow flowers in early spring. The leaves are somewhat fleshy and remain green in winter; in summer they are able to withstand long periods of drought without wilting. *P. auricula* is found mostly on rocks in limestone formations. Even though its habitat is moist for most of the year and its roots penetrate deep into rocky crevices, there may be a marked lack of water at times on the permeable limestone.

P. auricula grows mainly in the Alps from the Maritime Alps to Vienna abundantly, for instance, in the northern and southern limestone Alps. It is also found in the Juras and Schwarzwald, in the Apennines as far as Abruzzi and in the Carpathians. In the Alps it grows even at elevations above 3,000 m. Some sites, however, are located at lower elevations in the Alpine foothills — in some cases as relics of the Ice Age. Unusual is the existence of this species in a marsh north of Munich at an elevation of about 520 m.

P. auricula is one of the few alpine primulas grown with success in the rock garden. However, grown far more often for this purpose is the variously coloured hybrid between *P. auricula* and *P. hirsuta.*

Flowering period: IV—VII.
Perennial.
Height: 5—25 cm.
Leaves: Arranged in a ground rosette, up to 12 cm long, heavily powdered with farina.
Flowers: In umbels, 5-petalled, funnel-shaped, bright yellow with a white-farinose throat, fragrant.
Fruit: Globular capsule, 4—6.5 mm long.

Erinus alpinus L.

The genus *Erinus* has only the single species — *Erinus alpinus*. This plant is most abundant in the mountains at subalpine elevations; only rarely does it occur also in the alpine belt. Seeds of this plant may sometimes be washed down by water to lower levels and may catch a foothold in gravel deposits or in hill country at elevations of 400 to 500 m. It grows in rocky crevices, screes and on grassy patches on rock ledges. It is only to be found on calcareous rocks. In the Swiss Alps it occurs up to heights of 2,400 m above sea level. In the crevices of limestone rocks it often forms typical lime-loving communities together with *Potentilla caulescens, Hieracium humile, Festuca stenantha, Sesleria varia, Kernera saxatilis* and other species which require no more than a small amount of humus and fine soil for growth. The range of distribution of *Erinus alpinus* includes the mountains of northern Spain, the Pyrenees, the mountains of southern France, the Juras, western Alps, Apennines, Sardinia, the Baleares and the Atlas Mountains.

It is often grown in the rock garden where it does best in partial shade and light soil. The whole mass of plants may disappear entirely after the flowers have faded but they will renew themselves again from seed.

Flowering period: IV—X.
Perennial.
Height: 5—15 cm.
Stem: Erect, simple.
Leaves: Spatulate, roughly toothed, smooth.
Flowers: In clusters of 8—15.
Corolla: Of 5 unequal petals, the two upper narrower than the three lower, purplish-violet, rarely white or red, 7—15 mm across.

This is another primula of the *Auricula* section. It is closely related to *P. hirsuta,* for which it is sometimes mistaken. It differs, however, from the latter by the heavily powdered leaf margins, seemingly powdered flower stem and calyx, and more sharply toothed leaves. It is endemic to the western Alps, occurring only in the Maritime, Lepontine and Cottian Alps at elevations of 800 to 2,600 m. It is a calcicole and grows only in the rocky crevices or on the rock ledges of limestone formations. Another related species native to the western Alps is *P. allionii.*

The genus *Primula* contains more than 600 species, found only in the northern hemisphere. The focal point of their evolution is located in central and eastern Asia, mainly in the eastern Himalayas and western China. Most species produce two types of flowers. In the first type the style is the same length as the corolla tube and the stigma is furnished with long papillae on which only large pollen grains are caught. These pollen grains, however, are produced by the second type of flower; this has a short style and stigma with short papillae on which are caught only small pollen grains, produced by the flowers of the first type. Such an arrangement, known as floral dimorphism, prevents self-pollination.

Flowering period:
VI — VII.
Perennial.
Height: 5 — 12 cm.
Rhizome: Thick.
Leaves:
In a ground rosette, fleshy, sharply toothed, farinose margins.
Calyx:
Bell-shaped, farinose.
Corolla:
5-merous, pink to violet with a white farinose ring at the throat.
Fruit:
Longish-ovate capsule with flat seeds.

Yellow Whitlow Grass

Draba aizoides L.

Brassicaceae

The lovely golden-yellow blossoms of this plant appear soon after the snow has melted in certain mountain ranges. The dense, domed leaf rosettes, growing in rock crevices and screes, remain green throughout the winter. This makes possible for the rapid development of the flowers from the buds, already set before the coming of the winter season. In sunny weather the flowers are pollinated by insects but they are also adapted for self-pollination in the event of long rainy spells. Whitlow grass grows mostly on limestone and dolomite formations; it does not exist on acidic rocks. Its frequent companions on rocks are *Saxifraga paniculata, Primula auricula* and *Carex firma.*

It is mainly found in the Alps, Juras, Pyrenees, the mountains in the eastern half of France and Belgium, and in the Carpathians. Whether it is native to Great Britain is open to question.

The species is variable. Of the several forms best known are var. *aizoides,* found mostly at higher elevations in the Alps up to 3,400 m above sea level, and var. *montana,* with larger flowers and longer fruit stalks, growing mainly at lower elevations in the Alps and in the lower mountains of western and central Europe. An interesting characteristic of this species is that as the flowers fade they change from yellow to white. Because of the short growing season the seeds generally do not ripen until the spring of the following year.

Flowering period: IV — VII.
Perennial.
Height: 5 — 10 cm.
Leaves: In a dense, domed rosette, linear, leathery, bristly on the margin.
Flowers: In a 4- to 18-flowered raceme, 4 petals, golden-yellow, 4 — 6 mm long.
Fruit: 6 — 12 mm long, 3 — 4.5 mm wide, smooth or slightly hairy.

1 — fruit
2 — opened silicula

Rock Soapwort

Saponaria ocymoides L.

Caryophyllaceae

This genus is most widely represented in warm Mediterranean countries and the Middle East. Only a few species are adapted to high-mountain conditions, e.g. in the Alps *S. lutea* with yellow flowers and *S. pumila* with pink flowers, and in the Pyrenees *S. caespitosa*. The illustrated species is not exactly an alpine plant but represents an intermediate link between the thermophilous Mediterranean flora and the high-mountain species. It grows in the mountains of Spain, the Pyrenees, the mountains of Sardinia and Corsica, the Apennines, the mountains of southern and central France, the Juras, the Alps and the mountains of Jugoslavia. In the Alps it is found mostly to the south, its northward distribution being limited to the warm valleys. Nevertheless, it grows at heights up to 2,000 metres above sea level.

It multiplies easily from seed as well as by vegetative means so that it forms large mats on rocky slopes, dry screes, weathered limestone rocks and, sometimes, on river gravel. At subalpine level it grows amidst dwarf pine, at lower elevations in open pine stands. It also spreads along roads and railway tracks even in the lowlands and hill country north of the Alps. It is easy to grow even in larger rock gardens. Another soapwort commonly grown in the rock garden is the hardy hybrid *S. × olivana,* a cross between two high-mountain species — *S. pumila* of the Alps and *S. caespitosa* of the Pyrenees. *S. ocymoides* is closely related to *S. calabrica* which grows in the Mediterranean region.

Flowering period: III — X. Biennial or perennial.
Height: 10 — 25 cm.
Rhizome: Slender, branched.
Stem: Prostrate or ascending.
Leaves: Smooth, bristly only at the base, up to 3 cm long.
Flower: Densely hairy calyx, 5 petals coloured reddish-purple, rarely white, 12 — 18 mm long.

Chamois Grass

Hutchinsia alpina (L.) R. BR.

Brassicaceae

The white flowers of this species may be seen from spring until autumn and, when conditions are favourable, even in winter. This hardy plant was named after the Irish botanist Ellen Hutchins (1785 — 1815).

Hutchinsia alpina is found in the Alps on damp, mostly limestone screes at subalpine and alpine elevations, up to 3,000 m above sea level. The creeping stems branch profusely so that the plant is able easily to retain a foothold even in shifting stone debris. It multiplies easily from seeds, which are occasionally washed down by mountain streams to lower elevations. Here the plants grow on alluvial gravel together with other alpine plants washed down in similar manner, e.g. *Linaria alpina* and *Thlaspi rotundifolium*. In the northern foothills of the Alps *H. alpina* is found, for example, on alluvium deposited by the Lech and Isar rivers. Otherwise its range extends from the mountains of northern Spain across the Pyrenees, Juras, Alps (mostly the northern and southern limestone Alps), south to the Apennines and north-east to the western Carpathians.

Ssp. *brevicaulis* grows mainly on lime-free soil in the Alps, Balkans and Carpathians. Other species of this typically high-mountain genus are found in the Himalayas and mountains of Siberia.

Flowering period:
IV — VIII.
Perennial.
Height: 5 — 12 cm.
Leaves:
In a ground rosette, pinnatifid, smooth or hairy.
Petals: 4, white, 3 — 5 mm long, 2 — 3 mm wide.
Fruit:
4 — 5 mm long, 1.5 — 2 mm wide, with 2 — 4 seeds.

1 — flower
2 — fruit
3 — opened siliculae

Trumpet Gentian

Gentiana clusii PERR. ET SONG.

Gentianaceae

The genus *Gentiana* comprises more than 400 species found mainly in the mountains of the northern hemisphere and the Andes. Some, however, occur near the Antarctic in New Zealand, Australia and Tasmania. Some species of gentians are among the highest-growing plants in the world. For example, in the Himalayas *G. amoena* grows even above 5,500 m and in the Alps *G. brachyphylla* is found as high up as 4,200 m. Others withstand the rigours of the climate in the far north beyond the Arctic Circle, e.g. *G. tenella* in Greenland at 74°33′N. They are easily disseminated by the wind to great distances and heights for the seed is very light. Not every species, however, will germinate wherever its seeds are deposited for many live in symbiotic association with a particular fungus on their roots (mycorrhiza).

G. clusii grows mainly at subalpine and alpine elevations in meadows, pastures, screes and on rocks, with a partiality for lime soil. Its distribution embraces the Juras, Schwarzwald, central and eastern Alps, Carpathians and mountains in the northern part of the Balkan peninsula. In the Alps it may be found as high as 2,800 m above sea level; on the other hand it grows occasionally in valleys at an altitude as low as 500 m.

Flowering period: IV—VIII.
Perennial.
Height: 2—10 cm.
Rhizome: Short, unbranched.
Stem: Single-flowered.
Leaves: In a ground rosette, ovate-lanceolate, 2.5—5.5 cm long, pointed, leathery, wrinkled in dry periods.
Flower: 5-merous, trumpet-shaped, deep azure blue.

Buckler Mustard

Biscutella laevigata L.

This plant takes its Latin name *(bis* meaning two and *scutella* meaning small shields*)* from the shape of its fruits, which form pairs of adjacent flat circular pods resembling spectacles. Botanically this species consists of a series of populations which are difficult to tell apart. The morphological features are extremely variable, particularly the foliage, the toothing of the leaf margins and the branching of the stems. The most reliable distinguishing feature is the number of chromosomes. Some plants are diploid with 18 chromosomes, e.g. ssp. *kerneri* and ssp. *gracilis.* These are found mostly at lower elevations in the river valleys of central and southern Europe. Tetraploids with 36 chromosomes belonging to ssp. *laevigata* are found mostly in the Alps, Carpathians, Apennines and Illyrian mountains. In the Iberian peninsula there are even hexaploid plants with 54 chromosomes.

The most noteworthy form of high-mountain flora is ssp. *laevigata,* which grows at subalpine and alpine elevations up to about 2,700 m. Sometimes it appears alongside rivers down to the Alpine foothills where it may be found in the company of lowland forms. In the mountains it usually grows on grass-covered ledges of limestone rocks, often in spreads of blue sesleria.

Flowering period:
V—VIII.
Perennial.
Height:
15—40 cm.
Rhizome: Woody, polycephalous.
Stem:
Smooth or hairy.
Leaves:
Entire or toothed to pinnatifid.
Flowers:
4 petals, yellow, 4—8 mm long.
Fruit:
4—7 mm long, 7—12 mm wide with winged edge.

Apple-blossom Anemone
Anemone narcissiflora L.

Ranunculaceae

In early summer, when it starts to flower, the apple-blossom anemone is a beautiful sight on mountain meadows and grassy slopes. Its gleaming white blossoms are not borne singly as with other anemones (e.g. *A. baldensis* of the mountains and *A. nemorosa,* the wood anemone of lower elevations), but are arranged in clusters of two to eight. The fruits have a narrow membranous margin facilitating dispersal by the wind to great distances.

The apple-blossom anemone grows chiefly on limey soils but it is also found on siliceous soil. Its main distribution area is in the subalpine belt, whence it sometimes climbs to heights of 2,500 m in the Alps and Carpathians and even 3,000 m in the Caucasus. It may occasionally be found at lower elevations, e.g. in the Swiss Juras at about 600 m. Its range in Europe extends from the Pyrenees across the Alps, Juras, Vosges, Sudeten, Carpathians, Apennines to the Balkan mountains but its chief range is in Asia, from the Caucasus across Siberia to Kamchatka, Japan and beyond as far as North America.

The green foliage of this anemone contains the poisonous alkaloid protoanemonin which keeps it from being grazed by cattle.

Flowering period: V—VII. Perennial.
Height: 20—40 cm.
Leaves: Hairy, palmately divided into 3—5 segments, conspicuous involucre below the flower cluster.
Flowers: Long-stalked, arranged in clusters of 2—8, 5—6 petals coloured white, slightly violet outside.

Androsace ciliata DC.

The genus *Androsace* is closely related to the genus *Primula*. Some species look very much like miniature primroses. Primulas, however, have longish-cylindrical corolla tubes and are typically heterostylous; androsaces, however, have a short corolla tube with a narrow throat making it difficult for insects to enter, and its flowers are homostylous, equipped for self-pollination. The greatest resemblance to primulas is exhibited by the *Pseudoprimula* section of southeast Asia.

Best adapted to high-mountain conditions are the members of the *Aretia* section *(Androsace ciliata* belongs here*),* sometimes classed as a separate genus. They grow in high mountains from eastern Asia to the Pyrenees, sometimes even at the snow-line. They often make low cushions with long roots which anchor the plants in rock crevices and may live for several decades. The flowers are borne singly, not in clusters. The ripe fruits protrude only slightly above the cushions and are markedly hygroscopic. They open only in dry weather when the wind can carry the light seeds a great distance.

A. ciliata grows in rocky debris at alpine elevations in the central Pyrenees. It is closely related to *A. pubescens,* which is found both in the Pyrenees and in the southwestern and central Alps, where it climbs to heights of 3,700 m.

Flowering period: VII—VIII.
Perennial.
Height: 5—10 cm.
Leaves: Longish ovate, hairy, 6—15 mm long, pointed, petioles up to 15 mm.
Flowers: 5-petalled, pink or violet with orange or yellow eye.
Fruit: Globular capsule dehiscing by 5 valves.

Primula wulfeniana SCHOTT

Some high-mountain species are found only in a single mountain range and sometimes only in a very limited area in that range. Rich in endemic species are such high mountains as the Himalayas and the Tibetan mountains but the Alps also have their share. The illustrated *P. wulfeniana,* for instance, grows only in the southern Carpathians and in the southeastern limestone Alps, chiefly in the Julian Alps and Karawanken, where, for example on Hoch-Obir, it is found at elevations above 2,100 m. It generally grows at alpine elevations in grass together with *Carex firma* and other species such as *Gentiana froelichii* and *Silene acaulis.* It prefers damp soil and a snow cover lasting well into spring and supplying water to the soil as it melts. Sometimes it is found also in screes or on moist rocks but most exclusively on limestone. It may also occur at lower elevations in suitable spots in damp, shady and cool ravines.

Other species of *Primula* endemic to the Alps are *P. clusiana* of the northeastern limestone Alps, *P. spectabilis* found in the Alps of Verona, *P. tyrolensis* of the southeastern South Tyrolean Dolomite Alps and *P. glaucescens* found in the Alps of Bergamo.

Flowering period:
V—VII.
Perennial.
Height: 2—8 cm.
Rhizome: Short, sometimes branched.
Leaves: Rigid, dark green, glossy, glandular on the margin.
Flowers: In clusters of 1 to 3, petals joined to form a 7—14 mm long tube at the base, dark pink-red.
Fruit: Capsule, 6 mm long.

Alpine Whitlow Grass
Draba alpina L.

Brassicaceae

Draba alpina is the best known species of the *Chrysodraba* section. It grows in damp soil in stone fields, on rocks and in screes, beside snow fields and on heaths in the arctic and subarctic regions of Eurasia and Greenland. In the mountains of Scandinavia it is found up to 1,600 m above sea level; in western Greenland it has its northernmost distribution extending beyond the Arctic Circle to 82° 48′N. The Spitsbergen are the home of five other species related to *D. alpina,* of which only *D. glacialis* grows also in Norway and northern USSR. The only member of this related group found outside the arctic and subarctic regions is *D. ladina* growing on the limestone and dolomitic rocks of the Rhaetian Alps at elevations of 2,600 to 3,090 m. It is an endemic to the easternmost part of Switzerland.

The genus *Draba* comprises some 270 species, in the main characteristic plants of high mountains and polar regions. Many are perennial and make dense cushions, while some are sub-shrubs. The flowers are usually white or yellow but may also be violet. They are found in the high mountains of Eurasia, North, Central and South America, North Africa and on the islands of the arctic and antarctic regions. For example, *D. fladnizensis,* forming a group of about 25 small species, almost indistinguishable from one another, grows in the Alps, Pyrenees and Carpathians as well as in the mountains of Scandinavia and in northern Asia, the Himalayas, northern Greenland, Alaska, the Rocky Mountains and the Sierra Nevada in California.

Flowering period: V—VII.
Perennial.
Height: 5—20 cm.
Leaves:
In a ground rosette, elliptic lanceolate, entire, generally covered thinly with hairs.
Flowers: Yellow, with four 3- to 5-mm long petals.
Fruit:
Glabrous silicula.

1 — fruit
2 — opened pods
3 — flower

Androsace lactea L.

The genus was named *Androsace* in the Renaissance period. Originally the Greek word *androsakes* was the name given to an entirely different plant of the seaweed group found in the Mediterranean.

The genus *Androsace* includes some 150 species distributed throughout the northern hemisphere. The evolutionary centre of the genus is in the mountains of southeast Asia where the greatest number of species grow. Some, such as *A. primuloides* of southwestern China and *A. foliosa* of the Himalayas, are sometimes grown in the rock garden. The genus *Androsace* is divided into the following four sections: *Pseudoprimula, Chamaejasme, Aretia* and *Andraspis*. All hybridize easily — a clear indication that they are closely related. Members of the *Aretia* section have pedicelled flowers borne singly in the leaf axils, whereas the members of the other sections have their flowers arranged in umbels.

The illustrated species belongs to the *Chamaejasme* section. It grows in the crevices of limestone rocks and in limestone screes at subalpine to alpine elevations, occasionally at mountain elevations. Its range embraces the Alps, Juras, Illyrian mountains to Serbia and the Carpathians. In the Alps it is found at elevations up to 2,300 m.

Flowering period: V—VIII.
Perennial.
Height: 5—20 cm.
Leaves: In a ground rosette, linear, entire, glabrous.
Flowers: On 1- to 4-cm-long stalks in umbels of 2 to 6.
Petals: 5, white, 4—5 mm long, notched at the tip.
Fruit: Capsule with 5—10 seeds.

1 — fruit
2 — flower

Alpine Rose

Rhododendron ferrugineum L.

The name given to rhododendrons reflects man's admiration of their beautiful blossoms. Undoubtedly the choice, which calls to mind the queen of all flowers — the rose — was not accidental. The Latin name *Rhododendron* is derived from the Greek words *rhodon,* meaning rose, and *dendron,* meaning tree. The genus numbers some 700 species found mostly in the Himalayas, China, Malaysia, Japan, Kamchatka and the temperate regions of North America. Many have been in cultivation for years and many hybrids have been developed, some of which are even hardier and more beautiful than the parent species.

The alpine rose is a rhododendron of Europe's high mountains. Its range includes the Pyrenees, Alps, northern Apennines and the mountains of northern Jugoslavia, where, particularly on the northern slopes, it covers large areas. It grows above the alpine timber line (in the Alps up to 2,850 metres above sea level) and may also be found in open woods even at low elevations. Unlike *R. hirsutum,* which is a calcicole plant, it avoids limey soils. It is somewhat intolerant of cold and therefore grows in spots covered a long time with a thick layer of snow. The seeds are light — some 40,000 weighing only 1 g — and are easily dispersed by wind. The leathery leaves remain on the shrubs for three to four years and fall successively, so that the plants are continuously green. Grazing cattle avoid the leaves because they contain the poisonous andromedotoxin.

Flowering period: V—VIII. Shrub.
Height: 50—200 cm.
Leaves: Evergreen, leathery, entire, with rusty-brown, scaly glands below.
Flowers: 5-merous, bell-shaped, dark red, occasionally white, arranged in clusters of 6 to 12.
Fruit: Capsule dehiscing by 5 valves.

Alpine Clematis

Clematis alpina (L.) MILL.
Syn. *Atragene alpina* L.

This lovely ornamental plant, so popular in the rock garden, is the only twining and wreathing bush of central Europe's high mountains. Other twining plants of this genus, e.g. *Clematis vitalba,* occur in warm hill country. *Clematis alpina* grows mainly in light woods with fir, at the upper timber line with larch and cembra pine, in stands of dwarf pine and rhododendron, and occasionally in screes covered with fresh humus. It occurs both on calcareous and slightly acidic soils. In the Alps it is sometimes found as high as 2,400 m above sea level as well as in the foothills at elevations of 400 to 500 m.

Its range, however, is not limited to the Alps, it embraces the northern Apennines, Carpathians, and the mountains of the northern Balkans. Related *C. sibirica* is found in vast areas from Scandinavia across northern Russia and Siberia to northern China. Several other related species, which are sometimes regarded as forms of *C. alpina,* grow in eastern Asia and North America.

Clematis alpina and related species form only a small part of the large genus *Clematis,* which numbers some 250 species distributed in the northern and southern hemispheres from the tropics to the cold regions of the temperate zone.

Flowering period: VI — VII.
Twining shrub.
Height: 1 — 2 m.
Stem: Woody, bare.
Leaves: Opposite, long-petioled, trifoliate with ovate, toothed leaflets.
Flowers: 4-petalled, violet to pale blue, seldom white, petals 3 — 5 cm long.
Fruit: With 3-cm hairy appendage.

Globularia cordifolia L.

The genus *Globularia* comprises only about 24 species found mainly in the Mediterranean region, ranging westward to Madeira and the Canary Islands, eastward to the Middle East and southward to Somaliland. The species growing farthest north is *G. vulgaris,* which is found on the Oland and Gotland islands off the coast of Sweden and, outside its principal range, on the Iberian peninsula and in southern France. All globularias have blue flowers except for *G. nainii* of the Atlas mountains, which has yellow flowers.

The illustrated *G. cordifolia,* the same as *G. nudicaulis,* is found in the mountains of southern and central Europe. It grows in the Cevennes, Juras, Ligurian Apennines, in the Alps from Dauphine to Wiener Schneeberg, in the mountains of the Balkan peninsula and also in the Carpathians but only in the Velká Fatra and Low Tatra mountains of Slovakia. In the Alps it grows up to 2,800 m above sea level but is washed down by rivers to elevations of about 400 m, even lower in the south. This plant with its leathery, perennial leaves sometimes forms whole carpets on sunny rock faces and on stony screes. It prefers calcareous soil and is intolerant of excessive damp. Sometimes it grows together with *Erica carnea.* It is pollinated mostly by butterflies.

Flowering period: V—VII.
Prostrate sub-shrub.
Height: 3—10 cm.
Stem: Woody, branched, rooting at the nodes.
Leaves: In rosettes, petioled, spatulate, entire, leathery.
Flowers: 5-merous, with 2 short and 3 long petals, pale blue-violet, in terminal heads 10—15 mm across.

1 — cross-section of flower
2 — flower

1

2

Yellow Wood Violet
Viola biflora L.

Violaceae

The genus *Viola* comprises some 450 species distributed from the tropics to the cold regions of both hemispheres. Most are found in the temperate zone of the northern hemisphere and in the South American Andes.

Viola biflora is an important arctic-alpine plant found practically throughout the whole of the arctic and in most of the mountains of Eurasia and North America. In Europe it grows also in the mountains of the Balkan peninsula, Italy and Corsica, in the Pyrenees and mountains of Catalonia, in Asia in the Caucasus, Himalayas, in Japan and in Sakhalin. In the north its distribution in Asia extends far beyond the Arctic Circle to 70°N. In high mountains it is found far above the upper timber line, in the Alps, for example, up to 3,000 m and in the Caucasus up to 3,300 m above sea level. In congenial places, particularly alongside water courses, it descends to low elevations. In central Europe its lowest point is in the northernmost part of Czechoslovakia, in the sandstone formations along the river Elbe, at an elevation only slightly above 100 m. *Viola biflora* is a damp and shade-loving species which cannot tolerate dessication. The absorptive power of the roots is so low that the leaves wilt when atmospheric moisture drops. In winter it benefits from a long-lasting snow cover. It grows near springs, on wet rocks, in meadows with tall herbaceous plants, amidst the boulders of mountain streams and in swampy mountain woodlands. It favours basic soils but grows also well in soils which are slightly acidic.

Flowering period:
V—VIII.
Perennial.
Height: 5—12 cm.
Rhizome:
2—3 mm thick.
Stem: Ascending, smooth,
with 2—4 leaves
and 2 flowers
as a rule.
Leaves:
Broadly reniform,
long-petioled,
serrated.
Flowers:
Long-stalked,
bright yellow,
15 mm long, with
2—3 mm spur,
unscented.

Moehringia muscosa L.

The genus *Moehringia* is named in honour of the 18th-century physician and botanist P. H. Moehring of Ostfriesland. It numbers some 20 species, most of them found in central and southern Europe. Many areas where they are endemic are very small. For instance, *M. villosa* grows only in the mountains of N. and W. Slovenija, *M. dielsiana* only in the Presolana Pass in the Alps of Bergamo, and *M. diversifolia* in the southeastern Alps and western and central Jugoslavia. All these are very old relict endemics.

Whereas practically all moehringias have 5-merous flowers, those of the illustrated species are 4-merous. *M. muscosa* grows on shaded moss-covered rocks, in coarse screes and in cirques, almost exclusively on limestone and mainly at subalpine and mountain elevations. Sometimes it descends alongside rivers to lower levels. Its uppermost level in the Alps is 2,300 m. Below the alpine timber line it is found mostly in shaded, damp ravines. It grows in the mountains of northern Spain, the Pyrenees, Alps, Cevennes, Juras, Apennines, Carpathians and the mountains of the northwestern Balkans.

All moehringias have fleshy, fatty growths on their seeds. These are food for ants, which aid in the dispersal of the seeds.

Flowering period:
V — IX.
Perennial.
Height: 5 — 20 cm.
Rhizome:
Slender, fragile.
Stem:
Filiform, forked.
Leaves:
Narrowly linear, bright green, smooth, 1 — 3 cm long.
Flowers:
4-petalled, white, with 8 stamens.
Seeds:
Glossy black, up to 1.5 mm long, with fleshy growths.

Golden Cinquefoil

Potentilla aurea L.

This species rightfully deserves the Latin name *aurea,* meaning gold, for its flowers are deep glowing yellow in colour changing to orange at the base of the petals. It is found in subalpine and alpine meadows and pastures, occasionally also in stony screes and on rocks, and is very common in higher mountains. It is partial to acidic, siliceous soils. In lower mountain ranges, where there is greater competition from many other species, it grows also in limestone regions. It is found in various grass communities, mostly acidophilous — often, for example, in pure spreads of mat-grass *(Nardus stricta),* and in wind-exposed situations in spreads of *Juncus trifidus.* It will be found too in hollows and amidst dwarf pine where snow persists for a long time, together with *Calamagrostis villosa, Agrostis rupestris* and *Avenella flexuosa.* Its range extends from the Pyrenees across the central French highlands, the Alps, Juras, Vosges, Schwarzwald, Sudeten to the Carpathians, Apennines and to the mountains of Jugoslavia. In some places in the Alps it grows up to 3,300 m above sea level.

The genus *Potentilla* numbers more than 500 species found only in the northern hemisphere and extending as far as 70° N. Many species were introduced by man to the southern hemisphere. Related to *Potentilla aurea* is the arctic-alpine species *P. crantzii,* which is found mostly in limey soils, generally at subalpine and alpine levels.

Flowering period: VI — IX.
Perennial.
Height: 5 — 20 cm.
Rhizome: Thick, with rooting shoots.
Leaves: Basal long-stalked, palmate, 5-segmented. Stem short-stalked to sessile, trifoliate, with gleaming silver, hairy margins.
Flowers: 5-petalled, deep yellow, petals 1.5 — 2 × longer than calyx.

Rock Beauty

Petrocallis pyrenaica (L.) R. BR.
Syn. *Draba pyrenaica* L.

Brassicaceae

This small plant is an ornament of rock crevices, stony screes and talus on limestone and dolomitic foundations. It makes dense cushions of tiny leaves on woody stems and has a long root so that it can maintain a foothold even on steep rocks. In summer it bears delicate lilac flowers. It well deserves its name *Petrocallis*, derived from the Greek words *petra*, meaning rock, and *kallos*, meaning beauty. As the specific name indicates, it grows in the Pyrenees but is also widely distributed throughout the northern and southern limestone Alps and is locally found in the Carpathians in eastern High Tatra of Slovakia.

It grows mostly at the alpine level — occasionally at the subalpine; in the Alps in the region of Zermatt it grows up to 3,400 m above sea level. It is found in the same communities as yellow whitlow grass *(Draba aizoides)*, usually in the company of *Saxifraga paniculata, Hieracium humile, Kernera saxatilis, Primula auricula* and *Valeriana saxatilis.*

The genus *Petrocallis* is most closely related to the genus *Draba,* from which it differs by having the leaves three- to five-cleft and with simple hairs. Besides *P. pyrenaica,* it includes only one other species — *P. fenestrata,* growing in the Elburz Mountains of northern Iran.

Flowering period: VI—VIII.
Perennial.
Height: 2—8 cm.
Leaves: In a dense, ground rosette, 4—8 mm long, 3—5 cleft at the tip.
Flowers: 4-petalled, pinkish lilac, rarely white, petals 4—5 mm long.
Fruit: 4- to 6-mm long silicula, glabrous, with 2 (—4) seeds.

1 — fruits
2 — opened pod
3 — flower

110

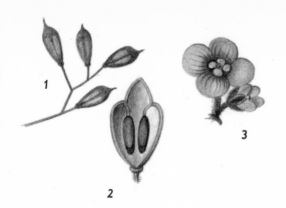

Least Primrose
Primula minima L.

Primulaceae

Primula minima, the smallest of all primulas, is also one of the loveliest with its glowing rose pink flowers rising from the centre of the small rosettes of leaves. In the mountains it often forms large masses in the alpine turf, on rock ledges and crevices. It is frequently found in dips and hollows where snow persists for a long time. It is partial to locations where the soil is wet in spring from melting snow. It grows in humous soil on lime-free foundations; if it does occur in limestone regions it will usually be found in slightly acidic soils on layers of humus or on interstratified beds of non-calcareous rock.

Its main area of distribution is in the alpine belt; in the Alps themselves it is found up to 3,000 m above sea level. Its range is disrupted, which indicates that this is a relict species. It is found in the eastern Alps, west to Brenner and Tonnale, in the Sudeten, western and central Carpathians and it has a scattered distribution in Serbia and Bulgaria. It often grows in the company of *Carex curvula, Gentiana frigida, Pedicularis verticillata,* purple saxifrage *(Saxifraga oppositifolia), Loiseleuria procumbens* and *Leucanthemopsis alpina.*

Unlike other primulas, the leaves of this species are wedge-shaped with 3 to 9 sharp points across its blunt end. The serration is variable.

Flowering period:
VI—VII.
Perennial.
Height: 1—4 cm.
Rhizome:
Much branched, polycephalous.
Leaves:
In dense rosettes, rigid, obovate wedge-shaped, up to 3 cm, sharply serrated across the blunt end.
Flowers:
5 petals joined into a 5- to 11-mm corolla tube. Whole flower 12—23 mm, bright rose pink.

Androsace carnea L.

One of the four sections of the genus *Androsace* is the *Chamaejasme* section, which numbers more than 30, mostly high-mountain species found primarily in eastern Asia. Only a few are found in Europe. Most widely distributed is the arctic-alpine species *A. chamaejasme* (rock jasmine), which grows in arctic and high-mountain regions throughout the northern hemisphere. The section also includes *A. lactea* and *A. villosa* of the limestone mountains of central and southern Europe, *A. obtusifolia* found on lime-free soils, and the illustrated *A. carnea*.

A. carnea is an extremely variable species growing in the mountains of central and southern Europe. It grows at alpine elevations, rarely at subalpine level, and in the Alps it may be found even above 3,000 m. It prefers lime-free soils which are very damp, especially in spring from melting snow. It sometimes makes large carpets in screes and thin grassland. It is found in the central Pyrenees and western Alps as far east as Simplon.

Ssp. *laggeri* occurs in the central Pyrenees, ssp. *rosea* in the Vosges, the mountains of central France and the eastern Pyrenees, and ssp. *brigantiaca* in the southwestern Alps.

Flowering period: VII—VIII. Perennial. *Height:* 4—12 cm. *Leaves:* In a ground rosette, linear lanceolate, hairy on the margin. *Flowers:* Arranged in clusters of 2—8, stalks up to 12 mm long, 5 petals joined to form a tube at the base, pinkish red to white with yellow eye.

Mountain Avens
Dryas octopetala L.

Rosaceae

Mountain avens is found in the northern hemisphere from Iceland and Ireland across Great Britain, Scandinavia, northern USSR to Alaska and from there south across the Rocky Mountains to Colorado. It also grows in the Pyrenees, Alps, Juras, Apennines, Carpathians, the Balkans, Caucasus and the territory beyond the Baikal. Its absence in the area between the mountains of central and southern Europe and northern Europe dates from the warm period following the Ice Age. The history of the area's geological evolution is 'written' in deposits from the glacial and post-glacial periods, which contain fossil remains of the leaves, fruits and pollen of what was then a very widespread plant. *Dryas* apparently formed a continuous belt in the tundra on the edge of the receding ice sheet together with creeping willows and the dwarf birch *(Betula nana)*. The gradual isolation of parts of the range resulted in speciation so that today there are a number of different species and forms.

Mountain avens grows chiefly on screes, rocks and moraines in limestone and dolomite regions often forming extensive carpets. In the Alps and in the Caucasus it is found at elevations up to and above 3,000 m but it will also grow at low altitudes, e.g. in Ireland and in the arctic regions by the seashore. In winter the green leaves are eaten by chamoix, red deer and reindeer, and to this day they are used to make a tasty tea in alpine countries.

Flowering period:
IV—VII.
Prostrate shrub with branched stem.
Height: 4—12 cm.
Leaves:
Oblong to ovate, leathery, serrate, glossy dark green above, white-felted below.
Flowers:
6—10 petals 10—18 mm long, white.
Fruit:
A head of achenes with long, persistent hairy styles.

1—multiple of fruits
2—achene

Alpine Aster
Aster alpinus L.

The number of species forming the genus *Aster* is not precisely known for it is sometimes difficult to distinguish between them and, moreover, certain species are sometimes classed in other genera e.g. *Linosyris, Tripolium* and *Bellidiastrum*. In the broader generic context it is estimated that there are some 400 to 600 species in all. The *Alpigeni* section, to which the illustrated Alpine aster belongs, includes low perennial plants, usually with a single flower head on an erect stem. The high mountains of central Asia and China are considered to be the evolutionary centre of this section.

The Alpine aster belongs to the alpine-altai flora. It grows in the Pyrenees, the mountains of southern France, the Juras, Alps, Apennines, certain central European mountains, the Carpathians, the mountains of the Balkans, the Caucasus, Urals, mountains of central Asia, Siberia as far as Kamchatka, and as a separate race (ssp. *vierhapperi*) in the northwestern parts of North America. With such a wide range it is only natural that the Alpine aster is very variable. There are two races in the Alps alone: ssp. *breyninus* with erect hairs and ssp. *dolomiticus* with appressed hairs. Alpine aster grows in grass, usually together with blue sesleria, and also in rock crevices, chiefly on limestone. In the Alps it is found up to and above elevations of 3,100 m.

Flowering period:
VI — VIII.
Perennial.
Height: 5 — 20 cm.
Stem:
Erect or ascending.
Leaves:
Basal spatulate; stem longish-lanceolate, entire.
Flowers:
Single flower heads 30 — 45 mm across on erect stems, violet blue ray-florets, golden-yellow disc-florets forming the centre.

Trumpet Gentian

Gentiana acaulis L.

Most gentians are deep blue to violet in colour, occasionally white. Only a few species are yellow (e.g. *G. lutea, G. punctata*) or purple *(G. purpurea, G. pannonica)*. A characteristic feature of gentians is that the corolla is curled spirally in the bud. Located at the base of the flower are so-called nectaria which produce a sweet liquid on which feed bumble-bees and moths with a long proboscis. These insects are the main pollinators of gentians. The flowers of some gentians are sensitive to vibrations and impacts which cause the trumpets to close more or less rapidly. All three species illustrated in this book close fairly rapidly. It appears that this response is a means of protection against the harmful effects of a sudden rainfall or strong wind.

The illustrated species, together with seven others, belongs to the *G. acaulis* group. It differs from the related *G. clusii* by having the inside of the trumpet spotted olive green; it differs, too, from *G. alpina* by having up to 10 cm long basal leaves whereas in *G. alpina* they measure 2.5 cm at most. *G. acaulis* grows in pastures, alpine meadows and screes on very moist and, above all, lime-poor soils. It is found in the Pyrenees, Cevennes, Juras, Alps, Apennines, Carpathians and Balkan mountains. In the Alps it grows up to elevations of 3,000 m.

Flowering period: VI—VIII.
Perennial.
Height: 5—10 cm.
Stem:
Single-flowered.
Leaves:
In a ground rosette, broadly elliptically oval, soft, entire, dull green, smooth on the underside.
Flowers:
Trumpets with 5 broadly ovate points, dark blue tinged with violet.

Sowbread

Cyclamen purpurascens MILL.
Syn. *Cyclamen europaeum* AUCT.

Primulaceae

The elegant form and the pleasant scent of its flowers make the cyclamen one of the loveliest of all flowering plants. The carmine-red petals are recurved, the throat is a darker hue and deflexed towards the ground, which makes the flower resemble a shuttlecock. When they have faded, the stalks curl in a spiral to make way for new flowers and to bring the globular capsules with the seeds closer to the ground. The sticky seeds are distributed by animals. The leaves generally remain through the winter. The entire plant, and particularly the corm, contains the poisonous glycoside cyclamin which can produce symptoms of poisoning in man. It is interesting to note that it is not harmful to wild pigs, which in some regions dig up the corms and eat them. In southern Europe the contents of the corms are sometimes used in bait when fishing in order to stun the fish.

C. purpurascens grows in stony, humousy soils, being particularly fond of limestone regions. It is most commonly found in light deciduous woods, often with beech and sometimes in coniferous woods. In the mountains it can be found up to elevations of 1,000 m, very occasionally also to heights of about 2,000 m. Its range embraces the Cevennes, Juras and Alps and extends to Moravia, Hungary and the mountains of the northern Balkans. Some eight other species of cyclamen are found mainly in the area between the eastern Mediterranean and the Caspian sea.

Flowering period: VI—X.
Perennial.
Height: 5—15 cm.
Corm: Globular or flattened.
Leaves: Reniform to roundish cordate, long-petioled, shallowly serrate, dark green with white spots above, reddish beneath.
Flower: 5-merous, pendant, carmine-red, petals 15—25 mm long.

Callianthemum coriandrifolium RCHB. *Ranunculaceae*

This callianthemum resembles certain white flowered alpine buttercups, chiefly *Ranunculus glacialis*. It is easily distinguished, however, by the number of its petals, from 6 to 12, whereas alpine buttercups usually have 5. As the plant matures the fruit stems lengthen and bend to the ground. The nectarias at the base of the flowers attract insects which pollinate them as they suck the sweet nectar.

The evolutionary centre of the genus *Callianthemum* lies in central Asia, where some ten species grow; in Europe there are only three. Best known of the Asiatic species are *C. alatavicum, C. sajanense* and *C. angustifolium*. Two species occur only in Japan; of these *C. hondoense* may be found at heights of as much as 3,000 m. Of the three European species *C. kerneranum* is endemic to the southern limestone Alps in the region of Lake Garda, *C. anemonoides* grows in the north-eastern limestone Alps in Austria and *C. coriandrifolium* is found on damp stony hillsides and meadows from Asturias across the Pyrenees, Alps to the Carpathians and the Dinar mountains. In the Alps *C. coriandrifolium* is found at elevations of up to about 2,800 m, in the Carpathians to about 2,350 m. It thrives in moist, humousy, neutral to slightly acidic soils.

Flowering period: VI—VIII.
Perennial.
Height: 5—20 cm.
Stem: Smooth, 1- to 3-flowered.
Leaves: Basal 2- to 3-pinnate, long-petioled, smooth, stem leaves usually 2, sessile, smaller and less divided.
Petals: Usually 6 to 12, white, sometimes pinkish.
Fruit: 3 mm long with pointed tip.

Alpine Pinks

Dianthus alpinus L.

Caryophyllaceae

Pinks are a beautiful sight both in the rock garden and in the wild. They fully deserve the name *Dianthus,* which is derived from the Greek words *dios,* meaning divine, and *anthos,* meaning flower. There are more than 350 species of pinks, all, with the exception of the arctic *D. repens,* growing exclusively in the Old World, mainly in the Mediterranean. Many of them are high-mountain plants, mostly those of the *D. alpinus* and *D. glacialis* groups of the *Barbulatum* section and some, e.g. *D. superbus,* from the *Plumaria* section.

Dianthus alpinus is restricted to the northeastern limestone Alps of Austria and to Italy and to Jugoslavia. It grows in pastures and meadows at subalpine elevations as well as on rocky slopes, mainly on a limestone base. It occurs up to elevations of 2,400 m. It sometimes forms large masses which withstand the competition of surrounding grasses.

Closely related species include *D. nitidus* of the western Carpathians, *D. scardicus* of the Illyrian Mountains and *D. callizonus* growing in the Carpathians of Rumania. All prefer calcareous soils. The high-mountain species of the *D. glacialis* group, found in the Alps, Carpathians and the Balkan mountains, have different soil requirements and are found mostly on siliceous rocks.

Flowering period: VI — VIII.
Perennial.
Height: 5 — 20 cm.
Leaves: Oblong to lanceolate, glabrous, 15 — 35 mm long, 2 — 5 mm wide.
Flowers: Single, very occasionally 2 — 3, unscented, broad bell-shaped calyx, 5 purplish-red white-spotted petals, 15 — 18 mm long.

Lloydia serotina (L.) RCHB.

The dainty little *Lloydia serotina* is one of the smallest members of the family *Liliaceae* found high above the upper timber line. Its whitish flowers adorn damp, mossy rock terraces, rocky slopes and firm screes where snow does not form large masses. The bulbs are usually submerged in the humousy debris filling rock crevices or in carpets of moss or in clumps of cushion-forming plants. The soil in such places is usually highly acidic and thus meets the needs of this species. It grows mostly on siliceous rock and when it occurs in limestone regions there is usually such an amount of undecomposed humus on the site that the influence of the limestone is negligible.

The plant was given its generic name in honour of the British botanist Edward Lloyd (1670—1709) who first discovered it in Great Britain. Its distribution there is local for it is absent elsewhere in northwestern and northern Europe. It is found in the Alps and Carpathians, the Balkans, Caucasus, in the mountains of Central Asia, in Siberia as far as Sakhalin, and from Alaska to Oregon and New Mexico. In the Alps near Mount Rosa it is found up to elevations of 3,100 m. It is a typical arctic-alpine plant.

The other 17 species of the genus *Lloydia* are found variously in Asia, mainly in the south-eastern Yunnan highlands.

Flowering period: VI—VIII. Perennial.
Height: 5—15 cm.
Bulb: Scaly skin disintegrates into fibrous remains.
Leaves: Basal linear, longer than the stem; stem linear-lanceolate, short.
Perianth segments: 6, whitish to pale lilac, violet-veined inside, 8—14 mm long.

Whorled Lousewort

Pedicularis verticillata L.

Pedicularis verticillata differs markedly from all the other plants illustrated here in that it is a hemiparasite, like all the members of this and related genera which form a separate, independent group — the *Rhinantheae* — within the *Scrophulariaceae* family. *Pedicularis verticillata* is green in colour and, as do other plants, derives its food directly from its inorganic environment; but with its roots it also absorbs water and the mineral substances contained therein from the host plant. Louseworts are generally parasitic on herbaceous plants, mainly grasses and sedges and other meadow and peat-bog plants, the illustrated species being most often found on *Sesleria varia, P. oederi* on *Carex firma,* and *P. palustris* on various other plant species.

The genus *Pedicularis* numbers some 600 species found mainly in the mountains of central and eastern Asia. Some grow high up in the mountains, others far beyond the Arctic Circle (e.g. *P. hirsuta* in Greenland as far as 83° 15′ N and *P. lanata* in Grinnell Land as far as 81° 43′ N).

The illustrated species is one of the most widespread. It is an arctic-altai-alpine species and is found in the arctic and subarctic regions of Eurasia and North America, in the Sierra Nevada, the Pyrenees, Alps, Apennines, Carpathians, the mountains of the northern Balkans, the Urals and the Altai. It grows in pastures and in damp rocky places, mostly in calcareous soil, in the Alps up to elevations of 2,800 m.

Flowering period: VI — VIII.
Perennial.
Height: 10 — 20 cm.
Stem: Erect, glabrous or with 2 — 4 rows of hairs.
Leaves: In a ground rosette, petioled, pinnatifid, those on the stem arranged in whorls of 3 — 4.
Flower: Beaked, purplish-red, 16 — 18 mm long.
Fruit: Ovoid, pointed capsule, 12 — 18 mm long.

130

Alpine Calamint

Acinos alpinus (L.) MOENCH

Syn. *Calamintha alpina* (L.) LAM., *Satureja alpina* (L.) SCHEELE

Lamiaceae

The genus *Calamintha* to which this species was originally assigned probably derived its name from the Greek words *kalos,* meaning beautiful, and *mintha,* meaning mint. The mint used in flavouring and cooking belongs to the same family and certain large-flowered species as well as the illustrated calamint are truly decorative plants.

Acinos alpinus grows mostly at subalpine elevations, though it occasionally may be found at alpine as well as mountain levels. It is very plentiful on sunny, stony hillsides, chiefly in limestone regions, but it also grows in siliceous soil. It is found in dry mountain meadows, open pine-woods and sometimes in rocky clefts. In the Alps it occurs up to elevations of 2,700 m. It is easily washed down by rivers to lower altitudes, where it may settle either temporarily or permanently on alluvial gravel. In some places, e.g. north of Munich, it has survived at this low altitude as a relic from the cold post-glacial or perhaps even the glacial period. It is distributed from the mountains of Spain across the Pyrenees, Juras, Alps, Apennines to Sicily, also in the Carpathians, Balkan mountains and even in Crete and the Atlas Mountains of Africa.

Flowering period: VI—IX.
Perennial.
Height: 10—25 cm.
Stem: Ascending, downy on the edges.
Leaves: Ovate to elliptical, toothed.
Flowers: In cymes in the axils of the upper leaves, lipped, bright violet, rarely pink or white, 15—20 mm long.

Purple Oxytropis

Oxytropis halleri BUNGE
Syn. *Astragalus sericeus* LAM.

Fabaceae

Purple oxytropis does not form large masses but is inclined to scattered growth. This occurs mostly in dry soil in thin spreads of grass as well as in alpine grasslands, firm screes and on rocks, often on mountain ridges exposed to strong winds. It has no particular soil requirements, growing in both calcareous and siliceous soil. It is generally found at subalpine and alpine elevations, in the Alps ascending up to 3,000 m above sea level, occasionally in isolated instances only at about 500 m, e.g. in the central Alps, where it sometimes grows in the company of certain thermophilous grasses. Its range of distribution embraces Scotland, the Pyrenees, the entire Alps, Carpathians and certain mountain ranges in the Balkans, where it occurs in several varieties differing for example in the shape of the leaves and other foliage.

The genus *Oxytropis* numbers some 300 species found mostly in western and central Asia. Some are steppe species which are distinctly thermo- and xerophilous, while others are markedly high-mountain species. Members of the genus *Oxytropis* have pea-shaped flowers with a sharply pointed carina (the lower part of the corolla formed by the joining of the two bottom petals).

Flowering period: VI—VIII.
Perennial.
Height: 5—20 cm.
Stem: Acaulescent with long, erect hairs.
Leaves: In a ground rosette, odd-pinnate with 8—16 pairs of ovate-lanceolate, hairy leaflets.
Flowers: In heads of 6—16, red or bluish-violet.
Fruit: Swollen, hairy legume.

Saxifraga cuneifolia L.

Unlike the cushion-forming species commonly found on rocks and screes at alpine elevations, *Saxifraga cuneifolia* grows mostly at mountain level. It will be found on damp rocks and screes in shady mountain forests with spruce, fir and beech, and grows up to the upper timber line. Only occasionally is it found at alpine elevations, more often it tends to follow river valleys down to low altitudes. It prefers acidic, siliceous rocks, occurring only rarely on limestone; when it does so, this will only be in soils with undecomposed humus. The plant contains saponin.

S. cuneifolia is a comparatively rare species in the Cantabrian Mountains, the Pyrenees and northern Apennines, growing mainly in the Alps and Carpathians. Closely related species find the oceanic climate of western Europe to their liking, and some have been cultivated as ornamentals for a long time. *S. hirsuta* grows in the mountains of northern Spain and southwestern Ireland. *S. spathularis* in the mountains of northern Portugal, northern Spain and in Ireland, and *S. umbrosa* is native to the Pyrenees. *S. hirsuta* and *S. umbrosa* are often found established in the wild in England and other countries of western Europe.

Flowering period: VI – VIII.
Perennial.
Height: 10 – 25 cm.
Leaves: In a ground rosette, leathery, smooth, oval, toothed, with yellow cartilaginous margin.
Flowers: On glandular stalks, 5 petals, white, spotted yellow or red at the base, 2.5 – 4 mm long.

Carex firma MYGIND

Sedges, of which there are some 2,000 species, greatly resemble grasses at first glance. In reality they belong to an entirely different family, differing from grasses both in morphological and phylogenetic aspects. Many species exist together in communities and form large growths in which members of other families often play a subsidiary role. Sedges are found mainly in the temperate and cold regions of both hemispheres, often far within the arctic regions or high up in the mountains.

One of the most common of alpine sedges is the illustrated *Carex firma*. It is largely to be found at subalpine and alpine elevations throughout the Alps, in the western Carpathians, central Apennines and mountains of northern Jugoslavia. In the Alps it occurs up to almost 3,000 m and may sometimes be washed down by alpine rivers to gravel terraces in the foothills. It makes extensive covers on rocky ridges and on the ledges and faces of limestone and dolomitic rocks, mostly in places exposed to strong winds which make it impossible for large amounts of snow to remain for any length of time. Only a few species tolerate such extreme conditions with their great fluctuations in temperature. *Carex firma* is the main component of the plant communities in calcareous alpine soils, where it grows together with *Saxifraga caesia, Silene acaulis, Gentiana clusii, Aster alpinus* and other plants.

Flowering period: VI — VIII.
Perennial.
Height: 5 — 20 cm.
Rhizome: Short, thick, branched.
Stems: In clumps, rigid, bent, thickly foliaged, bluntly triangular in section.
Leaves: Up to 5 cm long, 2 — 3 mm wide, smooth.
Spikelets: 2 to 3 pistillate spikelets, terminal staminate spikelet.

Round-leaved Penny Cress

Brassicaceae

Thlaspi rotundifolium (L.) GAUDIN

This penny cress with pale violet blossoms forms large carpets on damp, stony screes, mostly on limestone, only very occasionally on slightly acidic substrates. It has adapted to the inhospitable conditions of coarse stone debris poor in humus and good earth. Its germinating seedlings are capable of worming their way through a layer of hard rock fragments several centimetres in thickness. Its roots are anchored deep in the ground and its creeping stems branch profusely both above and below ground. Round-leaved penny cress is one of the main components of typical high-mountain communities which anchor screes. Other species often found in its company are *Hutchinsia alpina, Cerastium latifolium, Poa minor, Moehringia ciliata, Sedum atratum, Viola calcarata* and others.

Round-leaved penny cress is exclusively an alpine plant found in abundance in the northern and southeastern limestone Alps, occasionally on siliceous rocks in the central Alps and in the mountains of Jugoslavia. It is occasionally found above 3,450 m. Sometimes it is washed down by rivers onto alluvial gravel at lower elevations. Its somewhat fleshy leaves are eaten by the chamoix.

Flowering period:
VI — IX.
Perennial.
Height: 5 — 12 cm.
Stem:
Much branched, creeping.
Leaves:
In a ground rosette, finely toothed, the stem leaves alternate, entire.
Petals:
4, pale violet, 5 — 8 mm long.
Fruit:
7 — 11 mm long with 2 — 6 seeds.

Grim the Collier

Hieracium aurantiacum L.

Hieracium is one of the largest of all genera. Some 750 species, which interbreed easily and are difficult to distinguish from each other, grow in the northern hemisphere and in the Andes.

Most hawkweeds bear yellow flowers so that *Hieracium aurantiacum,* which grows in European mountains, is easily recognized by its bright orange blossoms. Its main distribution area is at mountain and subalpine level, where it grows mostly in meadows and pastures in poor, usually lime-free soils, rarely on limestone substrate. In the Alps it grows up to and above 2,600 m. It is also found in the Auvergnes, Juras, Vosges, some central European mountains, the Carpathians and the mountains of the Balkan peninsula. It is also found in the northwestern parts of the USSR and in Scandinavia.

Hieracium aurantiacum easily multiplies not only from seed but also through surface and underground runners. It is easy to cultivate in parks and gardens, primarily in rock gardens where it may develop into an unwelcome weed. This characteristic led to its reverting to the wild and becoming so established in various parts of Europe; it is, therefore, sometimes difficult to tell whether it is native to the locality or whether it has spread there. It is a variable species which includes about 35 different races and a great number of hybrids.

Flowering period: VI — IX.
Perennial.
Height: 20 — 40 cm.
Stem: Ascending or upright with 2 — 12 capitula.
Leaves: In a basal rosette and on the stem, longish-lanceolate, entire hairy and glandular.
Flowers: In capitula with 7 — 9 mm involucre, orange.
Fruit: Black cypsella with pappus of hairs.

Yellow Mountain Saxifrage

Saxifraga aizoides L.

Saxifragaceae

Yellow mountain saxifrage makes loose clumps beside springs, on moist screes and on alluvial deposits from mountain to alpine elevations. It also grows in places where snow persists until early summer. It favours basic, mainly calcareous soil, though it is sometimes found on neutral soil. A variable arctic-alpine plant, it is found in Iceland, the Spitsbergen, Great Britain, including the Isle of Man and the Orkneys, in Scandinavia, Novaya Zemlya, northern Asia, the Pyrenees, Alps, Juras, Apuan Alps, Carpathians, mountains of the Balkan peninsula, North America up to 80° N and in Greenland. Its main distribution area in the Alps is at heights of 800 to 3,000 m. It is also carried down to lower elevations along water courses. It was in this manner that it made its way down the Lech, Salzach, Rhine and Aare rivers to the foothils and down the Isar river as far as Munich.

Flowering period: VI – X.
Perennial.
Height: 5 – 20 cm.
Stem: Prostrate or ascending, covered with short hairs, glandular, branching at the base.
Leaves: Densely clustered at the base, narrow-lanceolate, fleshy.
Petals: 5, yellow to orange with orange-red dots.
Fruit: Ovoid globular capsule.

1 — flower

1

Alyssum alpestre L.

Alyssum alpestre grows in rock crevices and screes, chiefly on sunny southern slopes, and favours basic rocks. It is found in the western Alps from Upper Savoy in France to Wallis and Aostatal in Switzerland. At the alpine level it occurs at great heights, occasionally as high as 3,100 m above sea level. It is a variable species and its precise systematic delimitation is not wholly clear. Formerly it was linked with certain related species growing in the Mediterranean region, southeastern and eastern Europe, central Asia and Siberia, e.g. *A. tortuosum* and *A. serpyllifolium*. *Alyssum alpestre* is sometimes grown in the rock garden, as is the closely related *A. argenteum* of the southwestern Alps.

The genus *Alyssum* numbers over a hundred and fifty, mostly thermophilous and xerophilous species, distributed mainly in the Mediterranean region. Some, however, are typical plants of the high mountains, e.g. *A. wulfenianum* of the southeastern Alps and Jugoslavia, *A. petraeum* distributed from the eastern Carpathians to Macedonia and Istria, *A. ovirense* of the eastern and Dinaric Alps, and *A. cuneifolium* found in the Apennines, Pyrenees and Sierra Nevada mountains in southern Spain. In ancient times *Alyssum* was used to treat rabies — *lyssa* in Greek, hence the name of the genus.

Flowering period: VII. Perennial.
Height: 5 — 15 cm.
Stem: Thickly covered with hairs.
Leaves: Oval to lanceolate, hairy.
Sepals: 1.5 — 2.5 mm long, hairy.
Petals: 2 — 3.5 mm long, yellow.
Fruit: 3.5 — 4.5 mm long with 2 seeds.

King of the Alps

Boraginaceae

Eritrichium nanum (L.) SCHRAD. ex GAUDIN
Syn. *Myosotis nana* L.

King of the Alps is one of the loveliest of high-mountain plants. It greatly resembles the forget-me-not, particularly *Myosotis alpestris,* both in general appearance and the azure-blue colour of the flowers, so that it was formerly classed in that genus. However, it differs from the true forget-me-not in having the upper margin of the nutlets winged and not smooth.

The name of the genus — *Eritrichium* — is derived from the Greek word *eriotrichon* meaning wavy-hairy with reference to its striking foliage. It comprises some 30 species found in the mountains of Eurasia and North America. *E. densiflorum* grows in Asia on the world's highest mountain, and *E. villosum* in northern Asia far beyond the Arctic Circle. In all probability it is from the group of species related to *E. villosum* that *E. nanum* is derived.

King of the Alps grows at alpine and snowline elevations in the Alps, from the Maritime Alps to Niedere Tauern and Karawanken and in the eastern and southern Carpathians. It has a life-span of several decades. It is one of the highest-growing plants in the Alps, occurring even at heights of 3,750 m. It is found in rock crevices, occasionally in screes, and mostly on siliceous rocks. In the southeastern Alps, however, it is also found on limestone and dolomitic rocks. Though one of the loveliest of all rock-garden plants, it does not usually last long when grown in lowland regions.

Flowering period:
VII—VIII.
Perennial.
Height: 2—6 cm.
Root:
Strong taproot.
Stem:
Much-branched, densely-leaved, hairy.
Leaves:
In ground rosettes; both basal and stem leaves spatulate or oval, 5—10 mm long.
Flower:
5—8 mm across, glowing blue, rarely white, short corolla tube.

Edelweiss

Leontopodium alpinum CASS.

Asteraceae

The edelweiss is generally considered to be the symbol of the high mountains. It appears on countless souvenirs, ornamental objects, the badges of various societies and associations — in short, wherever there is some sort of link with the high-mountain environment. Its popularity, however, has also had an adverse effect on the edelweiss in that it was approaching extinction in certain easily accessible places. Fortunately this trend was halted by timely conservation measures and it is now a protected species throughout its entire range.

Edelweiss grows above the upper timber line in the Alps up to and beyond 3,100 m above sea level, mostly on stony soil, in the crevices of limestone rocks and in dry grasslands. Sometimes it descends down rocky river valleys to low elevations, e.g. along the Isonzo river in Italy to a mere 220 m. Its range embraces the Pyrenees, Juras, Alps, Carpathians and the mountains of Jugoslavia and Bulgaria. It is often grown in the rock garden where it does well in limestone debris. At low elevations or in humus rich soil, however, it loses much of its beauty.

The genus comprises some 30 species growing mainly in the mountains of central Asia and China. The sole European species has two subspecies — ssp. *alpinum* and ssp. *nivale,* which is restricted to Italy and the Balkans.

Flowering period: VII—IX.
Perennial.
Height: 5—20 cm.
Rhizome: Short, polycephalous.
Leaves: Linear-lanceolate, entire, densely white-felted.
Flowers: In terminal heads enclosed by many bracts making an irregular star.
Fruit: Cypsella with 4—5 mm pappus of hairs.

Phyteuma hemisphaericum L.

Phyteuma hemisphaericum is one of the best known representatives of the genus in the Alps. It grows in great numbers in poor, lime-free, acidic soils. In limestone regions it requires a thick layer of acidic humus on a limestone base; or where there is deep soil the basic substances must have been washed out in great measure by water. It grows in mountain meadows, pastures, screes and moraines, usually in the company of the sedge *Carex curvula* or in mat-grass areas on poor acidic soil. Occasionally, it occurs amidst dwarf pine or spreads of *Rhododendron ferrugineum* together with *Vaccinium uliginosum, Vaccinium myrtillus, Ligusticum mutellina, Leucanthemopsis alpina* and the like. In the Alps it grows up to 3,600 m above sea level. Besides the Alps it is found also in the Sierra di Guadarrama mountains in Spain, in the Pyrenees and in the Cevennes.

Like certain species of the families *Campanulaceae* and *Asteraceae,* the flowers of *P. hemisphaericum* are curiously equipped for pollination. The stamens, joined to form a tube, mature inside the corolla before it opens. As the style grows and pushes up through this tube, ripe pollen grains are caught on its hairy surface. Only when the style, terminated by a three-pronged stigma, has grown long enough to protrude from the flower can insects pollinate it from other flowers. Should pollination not happen the prongs of the stigma will curl until they touch the pollen-covered hairs on the style, thus pollinating themselves — a clear case of emergency self-pollination.

Flowering period: VII—VIII. Perennial. *Height:* 5—30 cm. *Stem:* Erect, smooth, leafless or with 1—3 leaves. *Leaves:* Linear, 1—2 mm wide, entire or with broadly-spaced, small teeth, glabrous. *Flower:* Tubular, with 5-pointed, dark blue-violet corolla, arranged in globular, terminal heads.

Alpine Poppy
Papaver alpinum L.

Of about 100 species of poppies only a few are perennial, mostly those growing in harsh climates, in high mountains and the far north. Most widely distributed is the alpine poppy. It is a variable species, the differences being mostly in the shape of the leaves and the capsule. The flowers are usually yellow or white, although they may occasionally be pink or red. The internal division of the species is complex. The limits of the many described taxa are disputed by different authorities and thus it is not always possible to make an exact classification of every specimen. In the Alps alone there are several closely related taxa, given here as subspecies of *P. alpinum:* ssp. *rhaeticum* and ssp. *kerneri* — mostly yellow; and ssp. *sendtneri,* ssp. *alpinum,* ssp. *ernesti-mayeri* and ssp. *tatricum* — mostly white.

Inasmuch as the alpine poppy occurs sporadically in other mountains, e.g. the Pyrenees, Abruzzi mountains, Carpathians, Dinaric Alps and Pirin mountains in the Balkans, and because it exhibits such marked variations, it may be considered an old species on the evolutionary scale dating from as far back as the Tertiary period. In the Alps it is most abundant at elevations above 2,000 m where the snow persists for a long time. Its highest point is 3,040 m in Unterengadin. It grows in shifting screes, mostly on limestone debris, together with round-leaved pennycress *(Thlaspi rotundifolium), Hutchinsia alpina* and *Linaria alpina.* Closely related species are *P. pygmaeum* of the Rocky Mountains of North America, *P. croceum* of the Mongolian Altai and *P. nivale* of the Verkhoyanski Mountains in Siberia.

Flowering period: VII — VIII.
Perennial.
Height: 5 — 25 cm.
Leaves:
In a ground rosette, 1 — 3 pinnate.
Flowers: Single, 4 — 5 mm across, 2 sepals which soon fall, 4 petals, white or yellow, occasionally red.
Fruit:
Capsule with appressed bristles 10 to 14 mm long.

Pink Cinquefoil

Rosaceae

Potentilla nitida L.

Most cinquefoils found in widely varied situations from lowland to snow-line in high-mountain elevations have yellow flowers, although occasionally these may be white. Red-flowered cinquefoils are rare and the illustrated *P. nitida* is one of these. It is not only the flowers that are noteworthy for the cinquefoil is an outstanding beauty on its own. All parts of the plant are thickly covered with appressed silky hairs giving it a silvery sheen. On sunny rocks and on gravel and stony screes at subalpine to alpine elevations it forms spreading mats of much-branched, woody rhizomes with many small, clustered leaves. It is particular as regards soil, growing only on limestone and dolomitic substrates.

P. nitida is found only in the southern limestone Alps, the western Alps from Dauphine to Savoy and Piedmont and sporadically, in the northern Apennines. In the Alps it occurs up to and above the snow line to heights of 3,200 m. Frequent companions are other similarly hardy species such as the sedge *Carex firma,* mountain avens *(Dryas octopetala)* and *Arctostaphylos alpina.* It is a very old, endemic species, the present division of its range having been caused by the ice sheet. Closely related to this cinquefoil are *P. alchemilloides* of the Pyrenees, the mountains of northern Spain and the High Atlas mountains, and *P. saxifraga* of the Maritime Alps.

Flowering period: VI — IX.
Sub-shrub.
Height: 2 — 5 cm.
Rhizome: Woody, branched.
Leaves: Mostly trifoliate with toothed leaflets and large stipules.
Petals: 5, red, very occasionally white, 10 — 12 mm long.
Stamens: 20.

Glacier Crowfoot

Ranunculus glacialis L.

Ranunculus glacialis is the highest recorded flowering plant in Europe. Its highest known situation is at 4,275 m above sea level on Finsteraarhorn in the Alps; others are not much lower. In the High Tatras it is one of the plants which grow at the top of Gerlach, the range's highest peak, at an elevation of 2,650 m. It is remarkable that this plant with fleshy leaves and stem withstands such low temperatures in a region of permanent snow and ice, anchored in damp rock crevices or growing in screes and moraines. It favours acidic soil on siliceous rocks; only rarely does it occur on limestone or other basic rocks. It is a typical pioneer plant, establishing itself on barren, perpetually damp rocks and boulder-strewn screes together with *Gentiana brachyphylla, Saxifraga bryoides* and *Androsace alpina.*

The leaves, foliage and colour of the flowers show marked variability. Like all members of the genus it contains the poisonous alkaloid protoanemonin. It is found in the Sierra Nevada mountains in Spain, in the Pyrenees, Alps, Carpathians, Scandinavia, Iceland, Spitsbergen and on the eastern coast of Greenland. The closely related species *R. chamissonis* is found only in the most easterly part of Asia and in Alaska.

Flowering period: VII — X.
Perennial.
Height: 5 — 20 cm.
Leaves: Basal stalked, stem almost appressed, fleshy, three-lobed and deeply notched.
Flowers: 1.5 — 3 cm across, 1 — 3 on a plant.
Petals: 5, white, later pinkish, persistent.
Fruit: Glabrous, beaked.

Red Alpine Catchfly

Lychnis alpina L.
Syn. *Silene liponeura* NEUMAYR
Viscaria alpina (L.) G. DON

Lychnis alpina is a miniature relative of *Lychnis viscaria* — a common and widespread species throughout most of Europe. The name *viscaria* (the Latin word *viscum* means adhesive) relates to the sticky bands below the nodes of the upper leaves of *L. viscaria* which prevent small wingless insects from getting at the flowers. The plant is generally pollinated by moths with a long proboscis; small insects would merely suck the sweet nectar without any profit to the plant. *Lychnis alpina,* though lacking the sticky bands, is closely related to *L. viscaria.* It has two types of flowers — hermaphroditic and pistillate. The pistillate flowers must be pollinated from another flower of the same species for fertilization to take place. However, even the hermaphroditic flowers are equipped for cross-pollination in that when the stigmas ripen the anthers in the same flower have already shed their pollen. The flowers attract insects not only by their glowing red colour but also by their pleasant vanilla-like scent.

Lychnis alpina is a typical arctic-alpine plant. It is found in the mountains of northern Spain, the Pyrenees, Alps, and, sporadically, in the Apennines, in Scandinavia, Great Britain, eastern Canada and Greenland. In the high mountains of Europe it grows on gravel, screes and dry pastures in regions where siliceous rock predominates. In the Alps it is to be found up to elevations of 3,100 m.

Flowering period:
VI—VIII.
Perennial.
Height: 5—15 cm.
Rhizome:
Polycephalous.
Stem:
Erect, unbranched, non-viscid, glabrous.
Leaves:
Narrowly lanceolate, bristly at the base, glabrous.
Petals:
5, pale red, 10 mm long, deeply slashed, with coronal scales.

Sedum anacampseros L.

The succulent-leaved sedums are divided into two groups — those with flat leaves and those with cylindrical leaves. *Sedum anacampseros* belongs to the first group, with *S. telephium* and *S. spurium.* It is a plant of subalpine to alpine elevations, occurring in the Maritime Alps up to 2,500 m above sea level. It grows on rocks, on old, weathered screes and on southern stony slopes already more or less covered with grass. It avoids calcareous formations and often forms large masses on acidic substrates. It is native to the Pyrenees and the southern Alps — from the Maritime Alps to the South Tyrol, and the Apennines. It was formerly grown as a medicinal plant. Nowadays it is to be found occasionally in the rock garden, so that it may occur in the wild even outside its original range of distribution.

Related species include *S. cyaneum* of eastern Siberia and *S. ewersii* of the Himalayas. Very similar to the flat-leaved sedum is the high-mountain *Rhodiola rosea* with dull yellow, sometimes reddish, 4-merous flowers. This grows in damp screes and in meadows beside streams from the Pyrenees across the Alps, Vosges, Sudeten and Carpathians to the Balkans, also in Great Britain, Scandinavia, Iceland, Greenland, Labrador and many parts of Asia.

Flowering period:
VII — VIII.
Perennial.
Height:
10 — 30 cm.
Rhizome:
Polycephalous.
Leaves:
Flat, oval, entire, smooth, densely crowded, particularly at the ends of sterile stems.
Flowers:
In globular heads, 5 petals, glaucous-lilac, occasionally white outside, deep dull red within, 4.5 — 6 mm long.

1 — open and closed flower
2 — fruit

1

2

Campanula pulla L.

Whereas most small bellflowers growing in the Alps are coloured various shades of blue, *Campanula pulla* is a deep rich violet. This species grows only in a limited area, mainly in the north-eastern limestone Alps; it is completely absent in the southern Alps. It grows with some abundance on stony grassy slopes and firm screes, sometimes even on damp rocks and beside springs. It prefers limestone and does not grow on siliceous rocks. It is to be found at elevations of 1,400 to 2,200 m above sea level, but occasionally may occur in a congenial spot at lower altitudes. All bellflowers are pollinated by insects; the anthers ripen and liberate their pollen before the stigma is ripe and this prevents self-pollination. When the fruit is ripe openings appear between the ribs of the capsules through which the small seeds fall as the fruit sways in the wind.

The genus *Campanula* numbers some 300 to 400 species found mostly in the mountains around the Mediterranean. The Alps are the home of several other small species of bellflowers, e.g. *C. cochleariifolia, C. excisa* and *C. carnica.*

Flowering period: VII—VIII.
Perennial.
Height: 5—15 cm.
Rhizome: Slender with underground runners.
Stem: Ascending or erect, single-flowered.
Leaves: Basal roundish-spatulate; upper lanceolate, smooth, bluntly toothed, slightly glossy.
Flower: Pendent, 5-petalled, deep violet.

Linnaea borealis L.

L. borealis is the only member of the genus which, like the genus *Erinus,* is monotypic. It is named in honour of the celebrated Swedish botanist, Carl Linne. *L. borealis* was his favourite plant and it usually figured in his portraits. It has a wide range of distribution in the subarctic and boreal regions and also partly in the temperate regions of the northern hemisphere. It grows in northern Europe from 71° 10' N to Scotland, Denmark, northern Germany and northern Poland, as well as in the Alps, Sudeten, Carpathians, Caucasus, the northern USSR to Kamchatka and Sakhalin and part of Japan; in North America it grows from the arctic regions southward to California and Pennsylvania and in southwest Greenland. In the mountains it is found only up to the upper timber line for its chief habitats are mossy coniferous forests, usually of spruce and pine, less often of larch, cembra pine and fir, and only rarely in deciduous woods of beech or birch. It prefers poor, acidic and moist soil with raw humus where, in addition to mosses, there grow blueberries, cranberries, *Oxalis acetosella, Homogyne alpina* and *Lycopodium annotinum.* Sporadic occurrences between its northern range and high mountain distribution in the temperate zone may be glacial relicts though the plant may also have been introduced there by birds.

Flowering period: VI — VIII.
Perennial.
Height: 5 — 15 cm.
Stem: Creeping, up to 4 m long, slender, woody, with ascending two-flowered branches.
Leaves: Opposite, round to broadly oval.
Flowers: Long-stalked, pendent, fragrant, 5-petalled, bell-shaped, white or pink.

Leucanthemopsis alpina (L.) HEYWOOD

Syn. *Chrysanthemum alpinum* L.

Asteraceae

The name *Chrysanthemon* was originally used by the Greeks for a number of herbaceous plants of the family *Asteraceae*. It is derived from the words *chrysos,* meaning gold, and *anthemos,* meaning flower. It has come, however, to be applied also to these white daisies with their golden-yellow centres. The genus numbers a great many species, from 150 to 300, and is nowadays usually divided into several smaller genera, e.g. *Leucanthemopsis, Tanacetum, Leucanthemum* and others.

Leucanthemopsis alpina grows in alpine grasslands, snow-filled depressions, firm screes and on the rocks of Europe's high mountains at alpine and snow-line elevations. It prefers siliceous rocks, growing far less frequently on limestone. With its perennial leaves it is adapted also to the brief growing season of localities above the snow line, often grows above 3,000 m in the Monte Rosa massif where it was even found at an altitude of more than 3,800 m. It grows in the Pyrenees, Alps, Apennines, Carpathians and Illyrian mountains. It is a variable species and several geographically different taxa have been described. They are distinguished mainly by differences in the shape and size of the leaves, the height of the plant and the foliage. *L. alpina* slightly resembles *Leucanthemum atratum*; the latter, however, grows only on a limestone substrate.

Flowering period: VII — VIII.
Perennial.
Height: 5 — 20 cm.
Rhizome: Short, polycephalous.
Stem: Upright or ascending, single-flowered.
Leaves: Wedge-shaped obovate, toothed to pinnatifid.
Flowers: Capitula 2 — 4 cm in diameter, white ray florets, with central golden-yellow disc.
Fruit: A ribbed cypsela.

Reticulate Willow
Salix reticulata L.

Salicaceae

Those who think of willows growing beside ponds and rivers in the lowlands will be surprised to learn that the genus, which numbers between 500 and 600 species, also includes dwarf shrubs only a few centimetres in height. These forms are adapted to the harsh climate of the high mountains and tundras. In the cold post-glacial period they grew in the lowlands of Europe near the edge of the ice sheet where, together with the dwarf birch *(Betula nana)*, mountain avens *(Dryas octopetala)* and certain other species, they comprised the vegetation of the tundra. As temperature gradually rose in the wake of the receding ice sheet, these plants were isolated in the high mountains or far to the north. Species found in both high-mountain and arctic regions (arctic-alpine species) include *Salix herbacea, S. reticulata, S. arbuscula, S. hastata* and *S. polaris.* Some species, however, are limited only to high-mountain regions, e.g. in Europe *S. retusa* and *S. serpyllifolia* and in eastern Siberia *S. fumosa* and *S. ramnifolia*; others are found only in the arctic tundra e.g. *S. arctica* and *S. rotundifolia.* In the northern tundra willows are a valuable source of food for reindeer because of their low cellulose and high protein content.

The reticulate willow grows in the arctic regions of Eurasia and North America, in Scotland, Pyrenees, Alps, Juras, Balkan mountains, Carpathians, Urals, Altai and mountains of eastern Siberia. In Europe's mountains it is generally found on limestone foundations, seldom on granite.

Flowering period: VI—VIII.
Prostrate, branching shrub.
Height: 5—15 cm.
Branches: Glabrous, brown, rooting.
Leaves: Roundish-ovate, entire, dark glossy green with impressed network on the upperside, with greyish hairs and prominent network on the underside.
Catkins: Terminal, appearing after the leaves.

1—staminate flower
2—pistillate flower
3—split capsule

Alpine Willow-Herb

Onagraceae

Epilobium fleischeri HOCHST.
Syn. *Chamaenerion fleischeri* (HOCHST.) FRITSCH

E. fleischeri is a typical alpine species found mainly in the western Alps. Its range extends from the Maritime Alps northeastwards to the line running from Garmisch-Partenkirchen, through Innsbruck and Gschlöss to Bolzano. Further east its occurrence is sporadic and in many cases it may have been mistaken for *E. dodonaei* which it resembles.

E. fleischeri grows chiefly in the gravel of mountain streams, stony alluvium and moraine debris, less frequently on damp rocks. In the alluvium deposited by high-mountain streams and rivers this photophilic plant forms typical pioneering alluvial communities. With its many underground runners it makes large masses which withstand not only the competition of other plants but first and foremost the ravages of flood water. It grows mainly on granitic rocks and crystallic schists, only occasionally on limestone substrates. Its main distribution is at altitudes above 1,000 m, though it is occasionally found as high as 2,700 m. In some places it grows on gravel deposited by mountain streams where they flow from the glacier, and sometimes it is washed down to low elevations.

Flowering period:
VII — IX.
Perennial.
Height:
15 — 35 cm.
Stem: Prostrate, ascending.
Leaves:
Linear-lanceolate, yellow-green.
Calyx:
Deep purplish-red.
Petals:
4, light purple, 15 mm long.
Style:
6 mm long, thick, crooked, white-felted half its length.

Cobweb Houseleek
Sempervivum arachnoideum L.

Members of the genus *Sempervivum*, as its name indicates *(semper* means always and *vivum* means alive*)*, will grow even under very unfavourable conditions for its fleshy leaves serve as a rich store of water. These plants may survive a dry period lasting several months. The very name of the cobweb houseleek specifies its characteristic trait — the cobweb-like hairs connecting the tips of the leaves at the top of the rosette.

Cobweb houseleek often makes thick carpets of sessile, tightly-packed rosettes on rocks, firm screes and dry grassy slopes. It prefers siliceous rocks, growing only occasionally on limestone. In the central Alps it is found at elevations of more than 2,900 m. However, it is not limited to alpine and subalpine elevations; in valleys it grows even at mountain levels and sometimes also in hill country. It is a variable species throughout its range, which extends from the Pyrenees across the Alps to the Apennines and Carpathians. It is often grown in the rock garden. Of the scores of species which make up the genus *Sempervivum*, many are high-mountain plants growing chiefly in the Alps and Balkan mountains — in the Alps, for example, the lovely yellow-flowering *S. wulfenii* and *S. grandiflorum* and the red and pink-flowering *S. montanum, S. tectorum* and *S. dolomiticum.*

Flowering period:
VII — IX.
Perennial.
Height: 5 — 15 cm.
Leaves:
Fleshy, in a semi-spherical rosette, glandular-hairy on the margin, otherwise sometimes nearly glabrous.
Flowers:
5 — 18 with 6 — 12 petals twice as long as the calyx, shortly pointed, carmine-red.

Blue Saxifrage
Saxifraga caesia L.

Saxifragaceae

Saxifraga caesia, belonging to the *Kabschia* section, is a typical example of the high-mountain cushion-forming saxifrages commonly grown in the rock garden. It forms thick cushions withstanding all the rigours of the mountain climate. The leaves are pitted with lime-producing glands covering hydathodes. Because it is so hardy this species will survive in exposed situations where even in winter the snow cover is swept away by the wind, e.g. rock steps and ledges, rock crevices and old screes at subalpine and alpine levels. There it often grows in the company of the hardy sedge *Carex firma,* mountain avens *(Dryas octopetala), Sesleria varia* and other species. In shaded gullies and ravines it may even grow at lower elevations below the alpine timber line. In the Rhaetian Alps it grows as high as 3,000 m above sea level. It has definite soil requirements, growing only on limestone and dolomitic rocks, sometimes also on amphibolitic substrate; it avoids acidic siliceous areas. As well as in the Alps this species is found in the Pyrenees, Apennines, Carpathians and Illyrian mountains in Jugoslavia. In the areas where it does occur it is common in all congenial locations.

The small seeds are noted for their ability to survive lengthy periods in water so that sometimes they may be washed down by streams and rivers to lower elevations, e.g. by the Isar river as far down as Munich.

Flowering period:
VII — IX.
Perennial.
Height: 4 — 11 cm.
Stems: In thick hemi-spherical cushions.
Leaves:
Rigid, recurved, 3 — 6 mm long, blue-green to pale grey, pitted on the underside with glands secreting calcium carbonate.
Petals: 5, white, 4 — 6 mm long.

Oreochloa disticha (WULF.) LINK

Syn. *Sesleria disticha* (WULF.) PERS.

Grasses are one of the most important families in the plant realm. Grasslands are natural formations capable of growing in all climates — for example, the bamboo thickets of the tropics, the flat, spreading steppes in all parts of the world, the many types of meadows and the vast beds of reeds in certain river deltas. Some grasses are among the hardiest of plants, e.g. *Poa arctica* and *Trisetum spicatum,* which grow far beyond the Arctic Circle in Eurasia and North America. Others grow on the coast of Antarctica and still others in the mountains above the snow line, e.g. in the Himalayas certain species of the genus *Poa* and in the Andes *Chusquea aristata.*

Several species of grasses form the predominating component of certain plant communities in Europe's high mountains at alpine elevations. For example, on siliceous rocks grow such species as *Oreochloa disticha, Agrostis rupestris, Festuca supina* and *F. varia,* on limestone *Sesleria varia* and *Festuca pumila,* and on acidic soils uniform spreads of mat-grass *(Nardus stricta).*

The illustrated *Oreochloa disticha* grows in acidic, humus-rich soil in exposed situations with only a short-term snow cover. It is found in the Alps and Carpathians; in the former at elevations even above 3,200 m.

Flowering period: VII — IX.
Perennial.
Height: 6 — 20 cm.
Stem: Rigid, slender.
Leaves: Bristle-like, smooth, up to 15 cm long, greyish-green.
Flowers: In two rows in a dense, ovoid flowerhead 10 — 15 mm long.
Lemmas: Keeled, bluish or yellowish.

Erigeron uniflorus L.

The genus *Erigeron* numbers some 350 species growing mainly in North America, but partly also in South America and Eurasia.

E. *uniflorus* is classed systematically with *E. polymorphus* and *E. neglectus* in the *E. alpinus* group. The group is variable and includes species practically indistinguishable from each other. This is further compounded by the tendency of all the species to hybridize.

E. *uniflorus,* an arctic-alpine plant, grows in the arctic regions of Eurasia and North America, in Greenland, the Pyrenees, Auvergne, the Alps, Apennines, Corsica, the Balkan mountains, Carpathians, Caucasus, on Ulu Dag (the ancient Mount Olympus) in Asia Minor, in Lebanon, the Urals and Tibet. Arctic plants are sometimes classed as a separate species. An unusual high-mountain aberration is the interesting form *nana* with reduced stem. E. *uniflorus* prefers neutral to slightly acidic soils on lime-free rocks and exposed situations at alpine elevations; in the Alps (Monte Rosa) it grows as high up as 3,570 m above sea level.

Flowering period: VII—IX.
Perennial.
Height: 2—15 cm.
Stem: Erect or ascending, hairy.
Leaves: Basal short-petioled, entire, with rounded tip; stem appressed, lanceolate, pointed.
Flowers: Daisy-like, 10—25 mm across, whitish to violet-tinged ray florets and yellow, violet-tipped disc-florets.

Marsh Felwort

Swertia perennis L.

The genus *Swertia* is named in honour of the Dutch horticulturist E. Swert. It comprises some 90 species with a world-wide distribution. In the temperate belt these plants are found both in mountains and lowlands whereas in warm regions they occur only in mountains. Swertias are the same to the high mountains of Africa as members of the genus *Gentiana* (belonging to the same family) are to the high mountains of the temperate regions of the northern hemisphere. For example, *S. kilimandscharica* grows from mountain to alpine levels 2,000 to 4,150 m above sea level not only on Kilimanjaro, as its specific name indicates, but also in other mountains in Tanganyika, Uganda, Kenya and the Congo.

The only European species is *S. perennis* which is sometimes considered as having two subspecies. The first, ssp. *alpestris,* has a stem measuring 25 cm in length at most and deep violet flowers 14 to 18 mm long; it grows along springs at subalpine and alpine elevations in Europe's high mountains, in the Alps up to 2,330 m above sea level. The second, ssp. *perennis,* grows up to a height of 60 cm and has dingy blue flowers 10 to 13 mm long; it grows in damp meadows from mountain levels down to the lowlands round the Baltic Sea, Lake Ladoga and in the Dnieper river region. Two other European species, the yellow *S. punctata* from the Balkans and the dark violet *S. obtusa* from the Urals, are now considered to be only colour variants or at most varieties of *S. perennis.*

Flowering period: VII — IX.
Perennial.
Height: 15 — 60 cm.
Stem: Erect, glabrous.
Leaves: Ovate to lanceolate, long-petioled, with prominent veins; upper semi-amplexicante.
Flower: 5-merous, greyish-blue to deep violet with dark spots and greenish throat.
Fruit: Ovoid capsule.

GLOSSARY

acidophilic — requiring an acid environment (acidic soil)

anemophilous plants — plants pollinated by the wind

basic rocks — alkaline rocks containing no silica at all or only a small amount, but often containing calcium carbonate or magnesium carbonate (e.g. limestone, dolomite, basalt, melaphyre, diabase)

biosphere — the zone of the Earth extending from its crust into the surrounding atmosphere, and containing living organisms

chamaephyte — plant with winter buds up to 30 cm above the soil surface

chasmophyte — plant usually found in rock crevices

cirque — circular recess confined by steep mountain walls made by glacial erosion; a natural amphitheatre

continental climate — climate where, because of lack of oceanic influence, temperature extremes are wide between the long cold winter and hot dry summer

cryophyte — plant which grows in ice or snow

cuticle — a delicate waxy layer over the outer surface of the epidermis of plants

cutinized cell membrane — a cell membrane impregnated with cutin

dealpine — alpine plant growing in the lowlands or hill country

deflation — erosion by the wind

denudation — process of erosion and transportation continually affecting the surface of the Earth. The main agents are water, wind, frost, etc.

ecosystem — a system made up of a community of animals and plants and the physical and chemical environment with which it is interrelated

endemic — a plant species occurring in a small, naturally limited region

entomophilous plants — plants pollinated by insects

erosion — wearing away of soil and rocks by water, wind or ice

glacial epochs — periods of geological time in the Quaternary period when the northern parts of Europe and North America were covered with glaciers

glacial trough — U-shaped trough or valley formed by a glacier

hemicryptophyte — plant with winter buds at the soil surface

high mountains — rocky parts of the Earth's surface extending far above the upper timber line to alpine or permanent snow levels

humus — organic part of the soil consisting of the remnants of dead organisms in various stages of decay

interglacial epoch — the warm and moist period between two glacial epochs

migration — spread of plants from one region to another

moraine — a mass of boulders and rock fragments deposited by a glacier

mycorrhiza — a symbiotic association of a fungus with the roots of higher plants

nunatak — an isolated rock protruding through glacial ice or snow and enabling the growth of living organisms

oceanic climate — climate influenced by the ocean; prevailing ocean winds bring clouds and rain in abundance and temperature fluctuations are negligible

oreophyte — mountain plant

orogenesis — formation of mountains through structural disturbance of the Earth's crust, especially by folding and faulting

papillae — tiny protruding growths from the epidermal cells

petrophyte — a plant living or growing on or among rocks

phenologic gradient — change in the rate of plant development in relation to altitude and longitude

photosynthesis — the production of organic substances from inorganic materials

psychrophyte — plant growing in cold and damp situations, chiefly in high mountains or tundra

range — entire region of occurrence of a particular taxonomic entity; the area occupied by a plant species

relict — a plant species living on in isolation in a small local area as a survival from an earlier period or as a remnant of an almost extinct group (e.g. a glacial relict is a survival from the glacial period)

saxatile — living or growing on or among rocks

self-pollination — transfer of pollen from anther to stigma of the same flower

siliceous rocks — rocks containing a large amount of silica (more than 65 %); the principal constituent is usually quartz (e.g. granite, gneiss, mica schist, phyllite)

snow line — the lower boundary of a mountain region in which snow never melts

solifluction — movement of temporarily thawed-out soil (with excessive amount of water) on a slope

spore-bearing plants — plants which multiply by means of single-celled spores (e.g. algae, fungi, mosses, ferns)

taxon (taxa is plural form) — a unit of systematic classification such as species, subspecies, variety

temperature gradient — the rate of change in temperature, especially with increase in altitude

tundra — plant formations in the far north or high mountains composed of mosses, lichens, hardy herbs and dwarf shrubs on soils which thaw out to only a small depth during the brief summer

upper timber line or alpine forest limit — line joining the uppermost points of continuous, uninterrupted forest

vicariants or vicarious species — closely related species occupying mutually exclusive areas

vegetational period — an uninterrupted period of favourable climatic conditions conducive to plant growth and development

wind-trained tree — tree with branches pointing in a leeward direction — in the direction of the prevailing wind

BIBLIOGRAPHY

Barnaby T. P.: *European Alpine Flowers in Colour.* 1967.

Hara H.: *The Flora of Eastern Himalaya.* I – II. Tokyo, 1966, 1971.

Hulten E.: *Flora of Alaska.* Stanford, California, 1968.

Huxley A.: *Mountain Flowers in Colour.*

Kihara H.: *Fauna and Flora of Nepal Himalaya.* Kyoto, 1955.

Polunin N.: *Circumpolar Arctic Flora.* Oxford, 1959.

Polunin O.: *A Field Guide to Flowers of Europe.* Oxford, 1969.

Polunin O., Smythies B. C.: *Flowers of South West Europe: a field guide.* Oxford, 1973.

Porsild A. E.: *Rocky Mountain Wild Flowers.* Ottawa, 1974.

Tolmatchev A. I. (ed.): *Vegetation of high mountain areas and its utilization.* Moscow, Leningrad, 1966.

Weber W. A.: *Rocky Mountain Flora.* Boulder, Colorado, 1967.

INDEX OF COMMON NAMES

INDEX OF LATIN NAMES